MIND YOUR HEAD

JUNO DAWSON

with advice from DR OLIVIA HEWITT

illustrated by GEMMA CORRELL

First published in Great Britain in 2016 by
HOT KEY BOOKS
80–81 Wimpole St, London W1G 9RE
Owned by Bonnier Books
Sveavägen 56, Stockholm, Sweden
www.hotkeybooks.com

Designed by Anita Mangan

A CIP catalogue record for this book is available from the British Library.

ISBN: 978-1-4714-0531-0
Also available as an ebook

7

This book is typeset in Century Schoolbook, Gemma Correll Font, True North Textures, Helvetica CY, Reprise Stamp, Dymo and Gill Sans

Printed and bound in Great Britain by Clays Ltd, Elcograf S.p.A.

Hot Key Books is an imprint of Bonnier Books UK
www.bonnierbooks.co.uk

Hampshire
County Council

Love your
Library

C016494571

CONTENTS

WARNING:

THERE'S ABOUT TO BE A TRIGGER WARNING.

THIS IS A TRIGGER WARNING ABOUT TRIGGER WARNINGS.

TRIGGER WARNING

This whole book is one great big stonking potential 'trigger'. There isn't a page in this book that won't resonate with someone. This book is intended to make you think and make you feel, not only about your own mental health and emotional wellbeing but about how difficult life sometimes is for other people too.

Some of the topics here do not make for comfortable READING, so you can only imagine what they're like to LIVE with.

Nothing has been included for the sake of gratuitousness. We're not trying to upset or distress people. If reading this book makes you feel wobbly or vulnerable, that is understandable, and probably normal, or means you aren't in the right frame of mind to be processing this sort of information just yet.

However, I also think those being 'triggered' by a book like this may need to read it most of all, as it aims to support, and features dozens of inspirational stories from people, just like you, who are living with, and indeed surviving, mental illness.

Juno Dawson & Dr Olivia Hewitt

CHAPTER 1

LETS TALK ABOUT...

OPENING UP ABOUT MENTAL HEALTH

LETS TALK ABOUT...

When I was at school, in the late Jurassic period, my friends and I became obsessed with a series of books in the library. They were large-format hardbacks called *Let's Talk About . . .* and each had a similar cover design: a teenager (in super eighties clothes – think what hipsters wear now, ironically) doing something with their hands.

In *Let's Talk About . . . Depression*, the girl had one sorrowful hand on her forehead. In *Let's Talk About . . . Anorexia* the girl was using her hand to push away a forlorn plate. In *Let's Talk About . . . Divorce* she had her hands over her ears while her parents fought. The less said about *Let's Talk About . . . Schizophrenia* the better . . . Hands EVERYWHERE.

They were very serious books and they talked about very serious things. This book is basically *Let's Talk About . . . Mental Health* and you can do whatever you like with your hands. Same issues, better cover.

SEXY DISEASES

Have you ever noticed how it's easier to talk about some medical problems than others? A broken arm or leg (while admittedly tricky to conceal) often comes with a zany skiing anecdote, and we make jokes about man-flu and hangovers. Crikey, some hangovers are so legendary they're almost badges of honour.

Some illnesses – the cancers, HIV and strokes – are talked about with deathly respect, while others – anything involving poo-poos and pee-pees – are considered crass to discuss. We get embarrassed and conscious other people might not want to hear about such problems over dinner.

But perhaps the hardest of all to talk about are mental illnesses. While we would all be quite happy to have people sign a plaster cast or bring us a lovely Lemsip, rarely do you hear people discuss their mental health problems. When people do, often they are met with little sympathy, considered weak, accused of faking – or worse, treated like a potential Jack the Ripper.

Have you ever heard the phrase 'squirrels are just rats with better PR'? Well, mental illness needed to hire a sassy PR person years ago. The reason people are reluctant to discuss their mental health problems in the way they might the flu, is partly a politeness issue (people are also funny about talking about diarrhoea or thrush, for instance) but also, I think, a public relations problem.

Think about the last time you read about mental illness in the news or saw it on TV. Was it a case of a crazed lunatic going wild with an axe, or a pilot flying a jet into a mountain? Was it a high-profile celebrity killing themselves? Was it some period drama set in a squalid asylum? I Googled 'mental illness in the news' and the top ten hits were all related to criminal cases – mentally ill people who had also committed crimes.

As with all news bias, if two unrelated concepts are talked about together enough, they become entwined in the collective consciousness. Clearly not all mentally ill people are going to commit crimes or kill themselves, but you can see why people have started to associate these two concepts.

The basic truth of the matter is that some diseases are sexier than others.

I think we all need to be more open about our mental illnesses. You see, I have a theory. Current statistics (many, many more statistics coming up, never you fear) indicate that one in four of us will experience some kind of mental health problem in the course of the year[1] but I think, IF WE WERE ALL HONEST, that statistic is probably more like four in four of us will experience some kind of mental health problem over the course of the year.

---

[1] Mental Health Foundation, 2014

I mean, think about the wording. A year is a long time. In the last twelve months can ANY OF US say we haven't been stressed, sad, anxious, angry, tired and emotional? I'm sorry, but if you're saying no, I think you're telling porkies. Honestly? HONESTLY-honestly?

I wonder if the issue stems from BLAME. Certain illnesses have different stigmas and I believe stigma often stems from blame. *Brass Eye*, a comedy show in the nineties, spoofed the media's treatment of disease with 'Good AIDS' and 'Bad AIDS'. Good AIDS was caught through blood transfusions while Bad AIDS was acquired through sex or drug use. The more we blame a victim for having an illness, the more SHAMED into silence they will be.

No one blames anyone for having the flu or getting cancer (unless you're a smoker, in which case you have BAD CANCER), but as mental illnesses aren't caught and spread like bacteria or viruses, blame falls on the victim. 'Can't he just cheer up?' 'Pull yourself together!' 'Why doesn't she just eat more?' Sometimes, with no external cause, and often no physical symptoms, people simply find it hard to make sense of, especially if they've never badly suffered.

Or if they PERCEIVE they've never suffered. Because of the media stereotype of the howling, strait-jacketed lunatic, it's no great surprise that many of us don't want to IDENTIFY as mentally ill – but what if we ALL are from time to time?

I don't understand why physical health and mental health are often treated as two separate entities (especially when they're so often linked). Our minds are not helium balloons floating some way above our bodies, held by a string. It's all in the one container.

So really it's not about physical health and mental health, it's about 'our health'. I think I might actually prefer 'WELLBEING' as a phrase, as 'health' is very tied up in medical thinking.

I reckon our wellbeing on any given DAY (never mind year) is a bit like the battery indicator on your phone. On your best possible day you'd be charged to 97% (because, let's face it, we're always a bit tired or bunged up or something). If you have a cold or a bit of a dicky tum you might be down to 50 or 60%. But then we MUST also add our mental wellbeing to this. So if you have a bad chest you might feel about 60% but you should ADD ON another hit for exhaustion after being up all night coughing – so you might really FEEL 35%.

Physical health doesn't just impact our mental health; it works the other way around too. Imagine you've got a massive exam coming up so you're super nervous (70%) and this leads you to get an upset stomach, taking you down to 55%.

How we feel mentally and physically are permanently intertwined.

Illness PERCEPTION is what varies from person to person. Basically, the percentage at which our battery changes to red is very much an individual thing. We adopt the 'sick role'[2] and take to our poorly bed when we PERCEIVE ourselves to be ill. For some of us that will be at 20%, for some it will be 35%, and some hardy souls not until 10%.

I would argue some of us only say we're ill if we have PHYSICAL symptoms, ignoring the depletion caused by mental factors, even though they drain our batteries just as much as physical influences do. That's a shame. If we were all more open about our overall wellbeing including mental factors, we could start to chip away at that shame and stigma.

That's one of the key aims of this here book. I want us all to come out of the mental health closet. I want us all to march in the mental pride parade. Turn to your neighbour right now and talk about a time when your emotional wellbeing has been less than 50%. I bet you anything he or she will be able to tell you about a similar time too.

Have you ever felt sad or low? Tell me about it.

---

[2] Parsons, 1951

Why did you get a copy of this book?

YOU & UR BRAIN

Now, this is where it gets more complicated. While we ALL experience periods of emotional turmoil or distress, some of us get STUCK there. It's like breaking down on the hard shoulder of the motorway – it's bleak and it's dangerous and it's scary. When mood resolutely refuses to 'perk up' after a period of time we move away from *emotional wellbeing* and into *mental illness*. We all have the potential to get stuck but we also all have the potential to get unstuck.

Clearly I am an author, and although I do have a . . .

FIRST-CLASS HONOURS DEGREE IN PSYCHOLOGY

. . . which I'm quietly proud of, I am not a doctor.

You should be very wary of writers and the like giving you advice on mental health – yes, even if they've suffered from mental health problems themselves. I've had a toothache, but are you gonna open up and let me perform that root-canal surgery? See my point?

The brain is the most intricate and unfathomable part of your body. Not even doctors know all its secrets, but they sure as hell know a lot more than I do. I am just here to share my experiences – which will hopefully encourage you to do the same – and present case studies of other people who are going through stuff too.

Luckily for all of us, I've drafted in the help of actual doctor and good friend Dr Olivia Hewitt, who is a clinical psychologist. She is on hand to explain all the SCIENCE BITS. Concentrate!

DR OLIVIA SAYS . . .

Why doesn't being told to 'get a grip' work? As one young person said: my friends told me to pull myself together and when I explained that I couldn't, the message I got back was just try harder.

To use a physical health metaphor, if someone had a broken leg and couldn't walk, would you just tell them to get over it? To try harder to walk? That wouldn't work because there is something biologically wrong. They need professional assessment and treatment, a cast, crutches, physiotherapy – you get the picture.

Similarly, people with a mental health problem have changes in their brain chemistry, which thus affects how they process information. Scientists have been able to show that completely healthy people experience these changes in brain chemicals when they are put in situations that mimic some mental health problems. So, for example, if we restrict the food intake of people who don't have a mental health problem, they start to develop some of the behaviour we see in people with anorexia nervosa.

While this means that, for some people, using medication to moderate the levels of certain brain chemicals is very helpful, it doesn't mean that medication is the only answer. Therapy can teach techniques to get our brains back to more helpful ways of processing information. Physiotherapy for the brain, if you like!

Don't be put off by us having a doctor listening in.
Let me share some facts about Olivia:

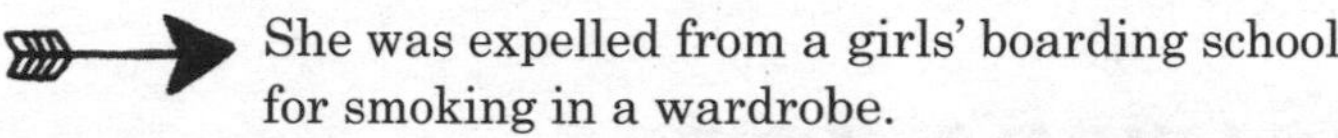

- She was expelled from a girls' boarding school for smoking in a wardrobe.
- At university, she wandered around town wearing a blanket. Yes, a blanket.
- She has a pet chicken called Fearless. Previous chickens include Feckless and Hapless.

A BEGINNER'S GUIDE TO BRAIN CHEMICALS

The brain is the most complex thing on the planet, and we are still learning about how it works. More than 100,000 chemical reactions take place in your brain every second. No wonder things sometimes go astray.

'The chemicals that allow nerves to talk to each other include dopamine and serotonin. **SEROTONIN** is thought to be particularly important in our mood – helping us to feel happy and reducing anxiety. **DOPAMINE** is involved in making people talkative and excited and can also be linked to forming addictions. Then there are **ENDORPHINS**, which can help us feel good and are produced in the brain in response to things like pain and exercise. When I think of endorphins, I like to think about tiny dolphins in my head. You're welcome.

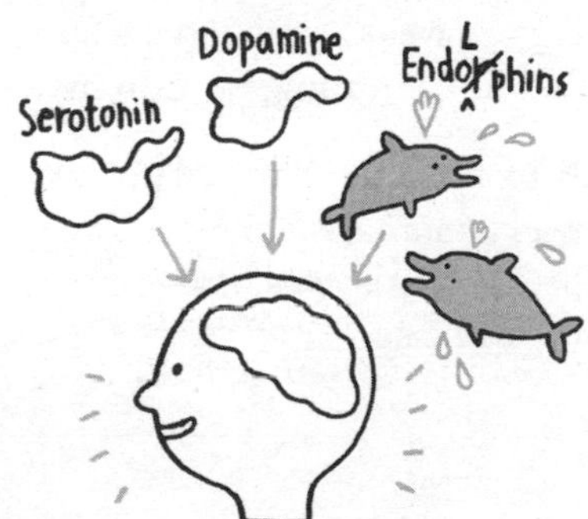

Our brain chemicals can be changed by what we do (like exercise), our environment, what we eat, and medication.

I'M BONKERS TOO

It's only fair that I share my own mental ouchies. After all, why would I be any different from anyone else? As I mainly associated mental health with depression or general SAD states I thought I'd got away with it, but alas no! Just because I rarely feel sad doesn't mean I don't have mental health issues. I wonder how many other people have low-level issues that we brush off as nothing.

Since I was about fifteen, I've suffered from irritable bowel syndrome (IBS). This is another not-sexy-but-very-common complaint that people do not like to talk about. This is where the mental part kicks in. Over the years I have developed great anxiety around my condition; the real punchline being that anxiety makes IBS about a hundred times worse.

Anxiety, although quite trendy at the moment, is far from pretty and/or desirable. My anxiety attacks feel like my skin is about to split open because my insides have reached critical mass. I sweat, I become unbearably hot, I can't breathe, my legs go weak, my head goes light, I can't stand or walk, and I feel like I'm going to poop myself in public.

It took me the best part of twenty years to recognise that there was a mental element to my problem. Yes, my IBS is a physical problem. Also yes, it is compounded and exaggerated by a mental issue.

PSYCHOSOMATIC ILLNESS: A physical disease believed to have a mental component resulting from the stresses and strains of day-to-day life. Common examples can include lower back pain, high blood pressure and IBS.

So there you go. Admitting my anxiety problem to myself was freeing. It has allowed me to manage my condition better, but more on that later. It took me a really long time to figure that out, probably because I was reluctant to even CONSIDER that it might be part of a mental health thing.

The aim of this book is to empower you to feel confident enough to seek the support you need, because we *all* need support from time to time throughout our lives. There are tips and ideas for living with and managing your emotional wellbeing. There are also stories from amazing, inspirational young people who are living with mental health issues.

This isn't a SELF-HELP BOOK because that phrase makes me cough up a bit of vom into my mouth, but also because I believe we all need a little outside help from time to time, but we can start by caring for ourselves a little better. That first step, for me, was admitting I needed help.

I always say this, but I'm also not a fan of being too precious about things. If we want mental illness to be treated in the same way as physical illness, we mustn't make mental illness in anyway special or unique. If we're able to make jokes about broken arms and bunions, we should also be able to make jokes about depression.

If you think mental illness is what makes you special, you are wrong. For one thing, millions and millions of people are suffering and for another there's no power in being a victim. Of anything. We become powerful through survival and endurance. A great way of empowering yourself is humour. Yes, in a tar pit of depression it's so, so hard to see the lolz, but dragging the gremlins out of your head and laughing at them is a sure sign of recovery. In fact, until you can talk about your mental health problems, I'd hazard they'll never get any better.

I'm not going to offend anyone with this book – hopefully – but I'm certainly not going to treat any mental illness like she's Queen of the Universe, because that's not how progress happens. If you're clinging to labels like they're Versace, I wish you well, I do, but I don't want to be anxious of freaking train journeys my whole life, so I'll be over here talking about how to beat mental illness.

CHAPTER 2

VITAL STATISTICS

A WORD ABOUT DATA

VITAL STATISTICS

There are lots of facts and figures out there about mental health. So much so, in fact, I'd wager that trying to piece together definitive numbers could drive you clinically insane.

For me, all the numbers you're about to see serve but one function: they exhibit how common mental health issues are. That's a good thing because I want you to see that you are far from being alone in the world. I think if we treat mental wellbeing as a continuum, with feeling a bit low at one end, incapacitated with poor health at the other and everyone else in between, the statistics would be even higher.

Nonetheless, let's take a look. As well as OFFICIAL DATA (capitalised for huge seriousness, obv), we carried out our own survey to find out how bonkers we all actually are.

First off, let's take a look at that OFFICIAL DATA.

 1 in 10 young people suffer from a diagnosable mental disorder – so in a class of thirty, that's three young people.[3]

 Approximately 1 in 15 young people deliberately self-harm.[4]

 Nearly 80,000 young people suffer from severe depression.[3]

---

[3] Mental Health of Children and Young People in Great Britain, 2004

[4] Truth Hurts: Report of the National Inquiry into Self-harm Among Young People. Mental Health Foundation, 2006

- More than half of adults with mental health problems received their diagnosis in childhood and less than half of those were treated properly at the time.[5]
- Anxiety affects 3.3% of young people.[6]
- Rates of mental health problems among children increase as they reach adolescence. Disorders affect 12.8% of boys aged 11–15, and 9.7% of girls aged 11–15.[7]
- 6.4% of adults display signs of an eating disorder. A quarter of those showing signs of an eating disorder are male.[8]

Remember – these statistics are often tied to hospital admissions and survey data, both of which are unreliable. I ALWAYS think that statistics are the tip of an iceberg. I'm not claiming to be representative, but my own anxiety issues have hung around since I was a teenager, yet I only sought help last year. I suspect there are lots of other people who would say the same thing.

---

[5] Prior Juvenile Diagnoses in Adults with Mental Disorder, Archives of General Psychiatry, 2003
[6] Mental Health Foundation, 2014
[7] Mental Disorder More Common in Boys, National Statistics Online, 2004
[8] Adult Psychiatric Morbidity Survey, 2007

THE MIND YOUR HEAD SURVEY

Dr Olivia and I were curious. Statistics are, as you well know, as slippery as an eel in baby oil. They must always be taken with a pinch of salt. We wondered how reliable statistics about mental health are, especially when official medical data comes from people who have accessed mental health services.

With this in mind, we carried out our own survey. Again, you are right to question statistics. Given that we approached people while writing a book about mental wellbeing, you can bet your bottom dollar those with a vested interest in mental health issues (i.e. sufferers) were the first to respond. With this in mind, we actively sought a mixture of people who both had and hadn't sought treatment in the past. Almost one thousand people responded and I think the results are quite telling.

- 86.6% of participants said that between the age of 13 and 19 they experienced some form of mental health/ emotional wellbeing issue. Clearly this is more than the suggested 'one in four'. In fact, it's more than three out of every four people in the survey. (See what I mean about stats – officially that's three whole humans and a leg . . .)
- Of those who DID experience some form of mental illness/emotional wellbeing issue during their teenage years, less than half (43.5%) sought formal support (i.e. a doctor, nurse, teacher or therapist). That, of course, means that more than half of the group received no formal support.
- However, 68.8% of those who experienced mental health or emotional wellbeing issues sought informal support, such as talking to friends, reading books or using the internet and chat rooms.
- Only 22.6% of the sample were prescribed medication to deal with their mental health or emotional wellbeing issues.
- About a quarter (24.8%) used alcohol or illegal drugs as a method to deal with mental health or emotional wellbeing issues.

Much as we predicted. If our survey is in any way representative of the population at large, it's probably a safe assumption to say that **there is an awful, AWFUL lot of people who are struggling with mental health or emotional wellbeing issues, and not all of them are getting the support they need.**

Bummer, right?

CHAPTER 3

DOCTOR, DOCTOR! I THINK I'M A PAIR OF CURTAINS!

ABOUT DIAGNOSIS

DOCTOR, DOCTOR! I THINK I'M A PAIR OF CURTAINS!

Now, as I've already suggested, our mental wellbeing fluctuates over time depending on our overall health, life events and brain chemicals so I'm in no position to say there's a definitive point at which a person should seek help for a mental health issue. Also, as health (mental or otherwise) is a personal experience, some people will require intervention sooner than others.

I think that we ALL need help from time to time to feel top notch. Be it taking a duvet day when you're stressed out, talking things through with friends over a lovely cup of tea, booking a massage or going to talk to your GP about feeling low/tired/stressed, we all need support. No man (or woman) is an island, and all that.

If you aren't feeling too great, it's important you talk to SOMEONE. I truly believe keeping it all in is only going to make things worse.

MEDICAL STUDENT SYNDROME

We need to talk about this for a moment. It's a recorded phenomenon that medical students are prone to a special type of temporary hypochondria whereby they start to believe they are experiencing symptoms of the diseases they are studying.

Mental health is no different, and, when reading this book or looking online, it might be tempting to leap out of your seat and scream 'EUREKA! THAT'S WHAT'S WRONG WITH ME!'

But that's not what this book is for.

You can't diagnose yourself, I can't diagnose you, and Dr Olivia can't diagnose you – unless she sees you.

The only people who can PROPERLY diagnose mental illnesses are GPs, psychiatrists and psychologists. Seeking medical help is covered in oodles of detail in the next chapter.

If you feel the accounts you read about in this book chime with your experience, that's totally normal and probably nothing to worry about. HOWEVER, I always think it's better to be safe than sorry and there is a lot of support out there. Talk to someone.

HOW ARE YOU FEELING?

Doctors use a highly complex measure to assess mental health when they first see you. It's called the *Diagnostic and Statistical Manual of Mental Disorders, Fifth Edition.* That's not very catchy though, so it gets called the *DSM-V.* It has to be complex so practitioners are able to diagnose patients correctly. The process is way more involved than a person turning up and saying 'I'm feeling low' and the doctor being able to make a definitive diagnosis.

It's important to remember that everyone has crappy days: days when you are FUMING because a bus driver didn't stop for you; days when you are so tired you cry watching those charity adverts (they often get me); days when you look in your handbag and find you have simply no figs to give about anything. None of these things mean you are mentally ILL, although they are days when your mental WELLBEING has taken a dent. Too many days like that and, yes, you could well end up stressed, anxious or depressed.

What a doctor or psychiatrist will look for is how long a mental situation has been occurring. Here's a very, very basic questionnaire that encourages you to think about your mood over the last two weeks.

1. Over the last two weeks, you've had little interest in doing the stuff you usually enjoy doing.

1 2 3 4 5 6 7 8 9 10

Disagree Agree

2. Over the last two weeks, you'd describe your mood as down, low or hopeless.

1 2 3 4 5 6 7 8 9 10

Disagree Agree

3. Over the last two weeks, you've had trouble falling asleep or have trouble getting out of bed (even on a no-school day!).

1 2 3 4 5 6 7 8 9 10

Disagree Agree

4. Over the last two weeks, you've lacked energy and feel tired all the time.

1 2 3 4 5 6 7 8 9 10

Disagree Agree

5. Over the last two weeks you've had little appetite or found yourself comfort-eating.

1 2 3 4 5 6 7 8 9 10

Disagree Agree

6. Over the last two weeks, you have felt like a bit of a failure at work, home or school.

1 2 3 4 5 6 7 8 9 10

Disagree Agree

7. Over the last two weeks, you've found it hard to concentrate on work or even things like watching TV.

1 2 3 4 5 6 7 8 9 10

Disagree Agree

8. Over the last two weeks, you've noticed a change in your mannerisms – you feel either slow and sluggish or buzzing and hyper.

1 2 3 4 5 6 7 8 9 10

Disagree Agree

9. Over the last two weeks, you've thought about harming yourself or thought about your own death.

1 2 3 4 5 6 7 8 9 10

Disagree Agree

10. Over the last two weeks, your mood has made it difficult for you to do your normal day-to-day activities.

1 2 3 4 5 6 7 8 9 10

Disagree Agree

Now, go back and do it again, only this time be less of a drama queen.

Kidding!

Now add up your score. Assuming you've been properly, honestly honest (after all, who's gonna see your score?) you should have a number between 10 and 100. I reckon we all probably have a score of about 20 to 30 as a base-level, but if your score is higher than 50, can you say why? Are you having one of those crappy spells we discussed? Like it or not, a crappy spell can last longer than two weeks. If you're going through a break-up or something, I'd hazard you'd be well over 50.

But if you CAN'T identify a life event or a reason why you might be feeling so blue, perhaps it's time to think about your mental wellbeing. Do the questionnaire again in another two weeks – has anything changed? A sustained period of low mood is clearly going to have knock-on implications for your life and overall health.

It could be that those cups of tea, massages or taking a couple of days off is all you need right now, but MAYBE it's also time to seek some support. As you'll soon see, there's plenty of it out there.

'When I was fifteen, I really struggled with depressed thoughts but was too scared to tell anyone for fear of them thinking I was weird or faking it. I'd seen a lot of things on the internet, particularly social media websites, stating that you can't be depressed unless a doctor has told you so. This put me off seeking any help for fear of being laughed at for being so silly.'

LEANNE 19 SCOTLAND

Some people often say that they felt their worries weren't bad enough to warrant seeing a doctor. This is nonsense. If you've been feeling off-it for a while, it doesn't matter what your symptoms are; a good doctor will listen and take you seriously.

A final word on diagnosis. Being told you have diabetes isn't going to sort out your blood sugar levels. Similarly, getting a diagnosis from a doctor isn't going to make anyone feel happier or less anxious. A diagnosis is the point when the real hard work begins.

Finally, not everyone is going to need a diagnosis – there might not be one to make – and not everyone is going to need formal, medical intervention. Support comes in all different shapes and sizes.

CHAPTER 4

HELP!

HOW AND WHERE TO FIND IT

HELP!

Let's get one thing straight: there is no shame or weakness in asking for help: in fact, it's the bravest thing we humans ever really do. It's also hard to first admit there's a problem and then to accept help.

If you go back to the last chapter and look at our little questionnaire, you'll see the last prompt was: *Over the last two weeks, your mood has made it difficult for you to do your normal day-to-day activities.* This is really vital. If the way you are feeling is making it hard for you to do normal things – go to school or work, see your friends or family, even getting up and showered – it might be time to seek support.

Perhaps the hardest thing we ever do is admit we need help. I almost typed 'admit we have weaknesses' but I actually think it's STRONG and CLEVER to ask for help when we need it. Pride and stubbornness are the real weaknesses here.

It might take a person a really, really long time to admit there's a problem, let alone ask for help. Remember, you wouldn't feel

any shame over a broken arm, and nor should you with a mental issue. Ever.

So something's up? Okay! What shall we do about it? Nothing, you say? Sometimes these things DO go away by themselves, but how many days do you want to spend hiding under the bed in the hope that this time they will?

It's far more sensible to seek help. Support comes in all shapes and sizes. Let's break them down into 'informal' and 'formal'.

INFORMAL SUPPORT	FORMAL SUPPORT
Friends	Your family doctor (GP)
Family	Psychiatrist/Psychologist
Websites	Medication
Other sufferers	Therapist/Counsellor
Books, TV shows and films	Teacher
Self-help	School counsellors
	Charities
	Social worker

The only real difference between these lists, as you can see, is one is of professionals and the other is not. For some people, informal support is all that's needed to see them through a period of anguish. But – and it's a big but – the people in the first column are NOT professionals and while we all need advice, love and care, much of the time we (and I include myself in this) don't have the faintest idea what we're talking about. What might happen when you seek informal support is they may very well point you in the direction of the second column. Something to bear in mind.

INFORMAL SUPPORT

I think when most of us are feeling a bit like we have mould on our brain the first thing we do is turn to someone we can trust, and this is a very good idea indeed. For me, it was my close friends. For you it could be a friend or a family member or even a teacher.

WRITE THE NAMES OF FIVE PEOPLE YOU FEEL YOU CAN TRUST

1. ....

2. ....

3. ....

4. ....

5. ....

FRIENDS AND FAMILY

We all need support from friends and loved ones whether we're having formal treatment or not. The only problem is that in the middle of a full-tilt 2007-Britney crisis we might perceive everyone and everything as against us.

That's probably not the case.

The good news is: even if you REALLY DON'T have a good shoulder to cry on, the professionals in the second column are paid to provide that service.

That said, it's nice to have friends and family to support you through tough times. It's very freeing to 'unpack the bag' and offload your worries into a sympathetic ear. Remember, everyone has bad days/weeks/months/years. Sooner or later, everyone is going to need a good old sob into a latte. Take it in turns! If you need help now, I bet my bottom dollar you've already been the supportive friend or will be in the future. In fact, if you open up about your problems with a friend, they'll be much more likely to open up to you.

Sometimes, having someone listen, or hearing from people who have been through the same things as you, can be hugely therapeutic. Just knowing you're normal is a powerful medicine. Well, hear this: whatever you're going through, you're 100% normal largely because 'normal' is an imagined ideal that doesn't really exist. It's a grass-is-greener thing – we see other people and covet their lives but, guess what, they're doing exactly the same thing.

Informal help can be an important first step to receiving more formal support. I guess we occasionally need 'permission' to make changes though; friends and family cannot 'fix you' – it doesn't work like that. You are the driver in the little car called Your Life.

WEBSITES AND ONLINE FORUMS

As everyone knows, if you're feeling poorly and type your symptoms into Google, you will almost certainly diagnose yourself with Ebola in seconds. Despite knowing that, it's far too tempting to see the web as the first port of call for any problem we have. How can we not? It's right there in our homes and it's totally anonymous. There are even fonts available that make things look OFFICIAL and FLAWLESSLY RIGHT.

But they're just fonts, yo.

Anyone could be writing that jazz. It could be your gran.

In fact, if MY gran was writing a website about depression she'd recommend what you needed was A GOOD WAR to put things in perspective.

What I'm saying is the validity and reliability of websites can be patchy. The NHS has some excellent resources and so do the mental health charities you can find listed at the back of this very book. All of those websites are absolutely the ones that CAN AND WILL help, and point you in the direction of further help if you need it.

LOOK! A HELPFUL WEBSITE!

Holly Bourne is a writer and relationship expert at YouthNet's TheSite.org, an information and advice website for young people aged (roughly) 16 to 25. They have over a million unique visitors each year in the UK.

'The aim is to help young people with absolutely anything that could go wrong in their lives. We have over 2,000 articles on everything from mental health and self-harm to sex and relationships, studying and housing. We also have peer-to-peer discussion boards that are moderated, and live chats with experts.

I work on 'Ask a Relationship Question', where a young person can ask any question about any relationship in their life – boyfriend, girlfriend, carer or friend – confidentially, and get a free response within three working days. People never have just one problem so our approach is holistic; we understand that if you're having a mental health problem your relationships will also be affected. Everything is linked and people want to deal with their issues in different ways.

Problems can be embarrassing – that's why people go to the internet – so everything is completely confidential and free. All the content is written by professionals and experts. I help people every day – you don't always see the results with it being online, but a lot of the time, I've seen TheSite save people's lives. We change lives. Sometimes people join us homeless or suicidal and by building a relationship with TheSite some of them have become peer mentors. They come full circle.

The internet can bring out the best and worst in a situation. With mental health issues, the internet can be a very unhealthy place. TheSite is a safe environment that is moderated and looked after by experts. We have very strict triggering guidelines in our community. We work with our users to provide a nurturing space and educate them on how to use the internet wisely.

Online support shouldn't replace face-to-face support when it comes to mental health. We're there as a crutch while people are on a waiting list or receiving other help, and we signpost users towards more formal help. We even have a section about going to your GP. The internet is not the whole answer.'

Vital Statistics: 89% of UK visitors to TheSite say it helped them feel better about their situation. The same percentage said the website made them feel calmer.

The Site is one of a number of moderated and professionally monitored websites that are 'safe' and have users' best interests at heart. Unfortunately, some corners of the internet are less... reliable. HOWEVER, I think this: if something is helping you and making you feel better, I think there's good in it. I'm not going to demonise anything that helps people.

'The internet was a huge help. Using journal-based sites wasn't only a cathartic way of getting everything written down, but it also introduced me to lots of people experiencing similar issues without any embarrassment or fear.'

'Tumblr helped me figure out what was happening to me, since I felt something was wrong but had never even heard of social anxiety before.'

ANONYMOUS 22 LISBON PORTUGAL

Using forums or social media to talk to other people who might be going through the same things as you is totally understandable because wanting to be understood is human nature. Speaking to other people who have experienced what you're experiencing can go some way to making sense of it and certainly reduce feelings of isolation.

'Most of my friends were made through chat rooms and forums, and the majority of them had mental health issues. They were a great help because they could talk from personal experience and some were available constantly if I was in a really bad place mentally. It's been almost five years and they still ask about how much I've eaten in a day because they worry, and will stay up until all hours talking to me. I definitely found these friends more helpful than the formal support. But sometimes my friends are less helpful or outright bad for me at certain times because of their own issues, which can be a problem. But we keep each other right, mostly.'

DANNY 19 NORTHERN IRELAND

The goal with any mental health problem is to reduce its impact on your everyday life. If using social media is enabling you to live a happier life, then I offer two enthusiastic thumbs up.

I do worry though, that some forums or websites are used a bit like a really gloomy echo chamber. By that, I mean a group of similar people reinforcing and celebrating mental health problems. Support – real support – isn't going to agree with you all of the time, I'm afraid. Instead of support it can be the blind leading the blind.

'Logging on every evening kept me going. When I thought of things during the day I wouldn't hear a voice, I'd see myself typing it out, and I dreamed in type. In hindsight I don't think it was really a great idea though, just hiding from the world, but at the same time I can't think of how I could have survived differently.'

Lots of people reaching out for support doesn't constitute support, and this is my concern with some online resources.

'On the whole it was a positive experience but as everything was tied around self-harm the environment itself could become triggery.'

The obvious examples are pro-ana (anorexia nervosa) and pro-mia (bulimia nervosa) websites and forums. I'm not judging anyone who might go on one; as we'll explore later, eating disorders are complex and often hard for non-sufferers to comprehend. Who better to talk to than other sufferers? If it's helping a sufferer make positive steps towards looking after their health (mental and physical) this is a good thing. However, if it's a collection of thigh-gap pictures, ribcages and comparisons of who can go the longest without eating, are we talking 'support' or is it simply 'enabling'?

ENABLER: A person who encourages negative or self-destructive behaviour in another.

Maybe that's where you're at. Maybe you secretly want to keep punching that big red self-destruct button – but that's a sign you need support, not the right kind of support in itself.

OTHER SUFFERERS

People with similar interests, be it *Doctor Who*, books or self-harm, are meeting up all over the internet.

Real-life support groups exist offline too. Sometimes like-minded people will arrange meet-ups themselves or do it through charities, such as Mind or Beat.

As with online forums, the plus is that you get to spend time with people who understand what you're going through as they may have gone through the same things. The drawback – as we saw above – is that sometimes the focus can switch from 'support' to 'competition', or can act as triggers for a lot of feelings. This is really unlikely to happen in groups that are facilitated, however, as the focus is very much on recovery.

BOOKS, TV AND FILMS

Suffering with any sort of mental wibble is likely to be scary if you don't know what's going on. Reading books or seeing characters on TV with the same issue can help to make sense of what's happening, and make you feel less isolated.

Media representation, while it still has a long way to go, is improving. Books like *The Bell Jar*, *The Catcher in the Rye* and *Prozac Nation* have been around for years; more recently, young adult novels like *Speak* or *It's Kind of a Funny Story* have now addressed teen mental health in a more modern teen-fictiony way.

TV and film portrayals are still few and far between, and often riddled with stereotypes, but films like *Silver Linings Playbook* do exist and handle mental health sensitively. Massive TV shows like *Girls* (Obsessive Compulsive Disorder) and *Homeland* (bipolar disorder) have also sensitively featured mental health storylines.

The danger with books, TV shows and films is that they can almost make mental illness seem aspirational. Clearly we know it is not. It's a bloody nightmare.

'I turned to books mostly for help. Not just "issue" books that dealt with the things I was going through but other happier books that allowed me to escape from my own problems. There was a non-fiction book about self-harm called A Bright Red Scream *by Marilee Strong that I came across by accident in my school's library. I feel strongly that this book saved my life. It was the first time I realised that other people were going through similar things and that there were other people out there in the world who also inflicted pain on themselves like I did. It was the first time in a really long time that I didn't feel so alone. After this, I sought out other books about depression and about eating disorders in order to help and educate myself.'*

'Nothing formal worked for me. I read a lot and listened to music, which helped more than anything else.'

SELF-HELP

By this I don't mean reading something from Oprah's Book Club (although that may be helpful). Instead, this section is about one of the most important things a human can do: LOOK AFTER THEMSELF.

We've established a link between physical and mental health. The better you look after your body, the better you will feel! This maintenance can be the first thing to slip when we feel a bit miserable, so it's important we don't forget these basics.

1. A GOOD NIGHT'S SLEEP CURES (ALMOST) EVERYTHING

Top tips for improving sleep:

- Try to see your bedroom as a calming sleep oasis. Limit other time spent there and, whenever possible, use electronics outside of this room. I KNOW, your room is your private place, but do you want it to be busy, chaotic and a social hub?
- Avoid caffeine after four pm.
- Establish a routine of going to bed and getting up, even at the weekend. Bingeing on sleep isn't healthy and nor is napping during the day.

If your sleep is broken and you wake in the night for more than twenty minutes, get up, leave your bed for a while, make a milky drink and do something calming until you feel sleepy again.

2. LET'S GET PHYSICAL

There is ample evidence that as little as thirty minutes of brisk walking a day will have the same effect as anti-depressant medication[9]. I'm a firm believer in fresh air curing all ailments, so put on some trainers and get out there.

LIST FIVE PLACES YOU COULD GO FOR A LOVELY WALK

1. ....

2. ....

3. ....

4. ....

5. ....

You may wish to avoid cliff faces and reservoir walks. Just saying.

---

[9] Blumenthal et al, 2007

However, there is also evidence that simply being among nature offers a mood lift[10]. How nice is that?

In chapter one, we talked about endorphins (remember the tiny brain dolphins?). These chemicals are released during physical exercise and also work to lift your mood. Now, no one hated PE at school more than I did so I feel your pain. The good news is there really is something for everyone. If you aren't into team games, try yoga, cycling or a gym. What better way than kick-boxing to release some aggression? You can also pretend to be Bruce Lee while doing it. The same is true of street dance and pretending to be Beyoncé. Even walking the dog or a leisurely swim will do the trick.

Now I appreciate that when a person is depressed, the actual LAST thing they want to do is attend a Zumba class, but think small steps. Even going outside and sitting in the garden or a park is better than nothing.

3. DIET

The key with diet is moderation. It's okay to have burgers and Coke, so long as these form a small part of your diet. Forget fad diets and trends, I'm talking about a diet containing all of the food groups: carbohydrates, proteins and fats mixed with plenty of fresh fruit, vegetables and water.

Eating well and regularly regulates blood sugar levels, which impacts on your mood. We've all experienced hangry spells, I'm sure.

---

[10] Thompson Coon, 2001

HANGRY:

The type of rage that can only come when someone ticks you off half an hour before lunch.

There are many, many, MANY studies that support the notion that poor diet (both eating little food or the wrong foods) leads to low mood, poor concentration and rapid emotional changes.

FORMAL SUPPORT

But what if you find it's not enough to have a moan to a friend? What if it FEELS like there isn't anyone in your life you can trust? What if their advice is well meant but vague? Is the internet panicking you? What if you actually prefer to do things in a more formal way?

Remember, a diagnosis isn't going to make you feel better or worse or validate what you're feeling, but it may be a relief to speak to a professional and have them give assurance, if nothing else. It bears repeating: this is all chemicals in your head. You're not at fault and there's nothing to be ashamed of.

GOING TO SEE THE FAMILY DOCTOR

For most people, the first step down a more formal path towards treatment is going to see their GP. Dr Olivia is going to talk you through the process.

DR OLIVIA SAYS . . .

You'd make an appointment with your GP. You do not need your parents' consent and the doctor has to keep it confidential[11]. There is no minimum age at which you can go to a doctor by yourself. If you're registered at a practice you can ask to see any GP you like, if you don't want to talk to your usual family doctor. Do you want them to be the same gender as you? Young or old? Your usual doctor or someone new? You can also request a double appointment so you have longer to chat.

Because mental health issues can be hard to talk about, you are welcome to take ANYONE with you – a parent or a friend. You may also wish to write things down in advance so you don't forget.

What are you concerned about? Do you have any questions for the doctor? What would you like to achieve? Medication? Therapy? You don't need to have any ideas, but some people do have a clear idea of what they want.

When you see your GP, they will ask you questions and it's important to be honest. Remember, they've heard it ALL before! You might meet a GP who is less than helpful. This could be because they trained a long time ago or have little experience in dealing with mental health issues. DO NOT let this put you off – see another doctor as soon as you can. Finding a GP you can trust is vital for all health matters.

What happens next depends on the GP, what you told them and what's available in your local area.

---

[11] Throughout contact with all mental health professionals there are limits to confidentiality. You might want to check what these are with the person before you start talking to them. They tend to be around risk and harm, so people will break confidentiality if they feel you or someone else is likely to be harmed.

Some outcomes could be:

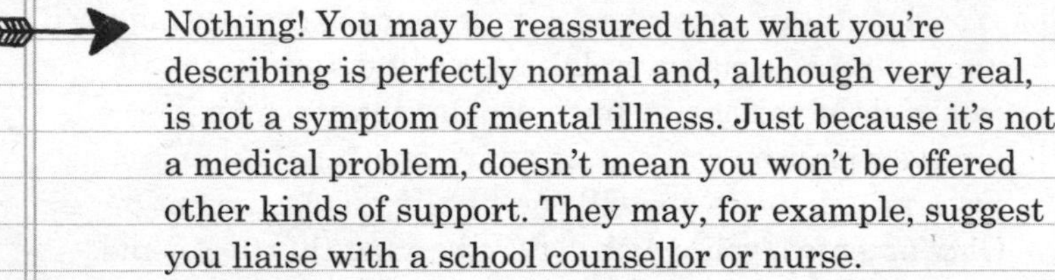

- Nothing! You may be reassured that what you're describing is perfectly normal and, although very real, is not a symptom of mental illness. Just because it's not a medical problem, doesn't mean you won't be offered other kinds of support. They may, for example, suggest you liaise with a school counsellor or nurse.

- Watchful waiting. This is when your GP will ask you to come back in a couple of weeks to see whether things have changed.

- Medication. After a period of watchful waiting you may be offered some medication.

- You might be told about other services, such as school counsellors, charities or organisations.

- CAMHS (see below).

- If there is a Primary Care Service in your area, you might be referred to them – they are similar to CAMHS, but have a lower entry threshold.

For people under the age of eighteen, your specialist team is CAMHS (Children and Adolescent Mental Health Service). This is a multi-disciplinary team of nurses, psychiatrists, psychologists and other professionals. Waiting lists can be quite long and it can be hard to access this service, but don't let that put you off. In some parts of the country, a primary mental healthcare service for young people are being trialled as an alternative.

If you are referred to CAMHS, you might be sent some questionnaires so they can gain a better understanding of your difficulties. You could be offered an assessment appointment or put on a waiting list and sent self-help material. At this stage, some people require no further intervention.

Once accepted, you may be offered a range of treatments, such as attending a group facilitated by a professional, being prescribed medication by a psychiatrist or individual therapy.

For over eighteens, there are community mental health teams, which function in a similar way to a CAMHS team. Most adults would initially be referred to IAPT (Improved Access to Psychological Therapies), which have many different names depending on your local area. This service promotes 'talking therapies' over medication, although your GP may prescribe medication alongside.

Very, very rarely, people are so poorly they need to bc in hospital while they receive their treatment. This only usually happens after other community-based treatments have been tried. If you are under eighteen, you would be admitted to a specialist young person's ward.

A note on 'sectioning'. On some VERY rare occasions, people need to be treated against their will. This process is controlled by the law and has legal safeguards built in so it can't be used inappropriately. People are detained under the Mental Health Act (usually section 2 or 3 – hence the term 'to be sectioned'). This can only happen if two mental health professionals believe it is necessary and can't happen in any other way.

Let's clarify some of what Dr Olivia just told us.

WHO ARE THESE PEOPLE?

A GP: A general practitioner, or family doctor. They can prescribe you medication and may refer you on to more specialist services.

PSYCHIATRIST: This is a doctor who has had medical training and then specialised in mental illness. They can also prescribe medication and diagnose mental illness.

PSYCHOLOGIST: These people are also doctors, but not medical doctors. This means they don't prescribe medication, but do provide therapy.

If you've felt rubbish for a while and informal support isn't making you feel any better, it's important to see a doctor, even if you're not a fan of hospitals and clinics. As we've said many times, you wouldn't drag a gangrenous leg around town and nor should you drag a gangrenous brain. Some physical problems also mimic mental health problems. For instance, a thyroid issue or a urinary tract infection can have a lot of the same symptoms as depression so it's important to rule these out before even starting a dialogue about mental illness.

We must seek to banish myths about doctors, medication and therapy just as much as we need to reduce stigma around mental illness. The two often go hand in hand.

'I was grateful to have a GP that understood and was willing to provide immediate help. He apologised for the waiting list to see the therapy specialist but gave me reading material and promised that things would get better. He didn't give me medication, saying that he had faith I could do it without, but promised that if I ever felt I was out of control he would provide it for me.'

'The first doctor I spoke to laughed and told me to stop doing it [self-harm]. The second doctor prescribed me medication, was understanding and referred me to relaxation classes, which really helped.'

THERAPY

There are lots of different kinds of therapy and it's important that, if the first one you try doesn't work for you, you find one that does. There are therapies focused on different activities, such as music, drama and art. The most common type of therapy is talking therapy. This can happen in a group or one to one. Again, there are lots of different styles of talking therapy. One you might have heard of is cognitive behavioural therapy (CBT). This looks at our thoughts and behaviour and uses these to change our mood.

TRY THIS EXERCISE

Imagine you are awakened in the night by the sound of glass smashing . . .

You think 'it's a **burglar**'. How **likely** is this? What **emotion** would you feel? What would you **do**?

Now imagine you are awakened in the night by the sound of glass smashing . . .

You think 'the **cat** knocked over the milk bottles'. How **likely** is THIS? What **emotion** would you feel? What would you **do**?

Hopefully you can see that our thoughts lead to different emotions and different responses. This is what CBT focuses on – unpinning and unravelling destructive thought processes. It generally looks at the 'here and now', or mindfulness, to see what practical changes can be made to help you feel better.

'I received anti-depressants and anti-psychotic medications at age seventeen, which had a detrimental effect on my wellbeing. It felt as though I was walking around in a haze for months. After taking myself off the drugs, I was offered CBT. CBT was excellent and gave me confidence and temporarily relieved me of my anxiety. I have been able to use the breathing techniques I learned in CBT to control my anxiety.'

Other types of therapy are focused on developing a safe relationship with a counsellor who can then help you to explore how you are feeling and why these feelings might have developed over time.

A word about groups. Some people are really scared about joining a therapy group. They might feel worried about what the other people in the group will think about them, or feel that the group might not focus on what they need. However, groups can be super helpful because they allow you to meet other people who have similar difficulties to you (making you feel less alone and isolated) and you can learn from other people what works for them. Also, the other people in the group were probably just as nervous to start off with, understand how tricky it is to be the newby, and will be super supportive!

MEDICATION

In some cases, a GP or a psychiatrist may prescribe medication. Some common medications you might have heard of are:

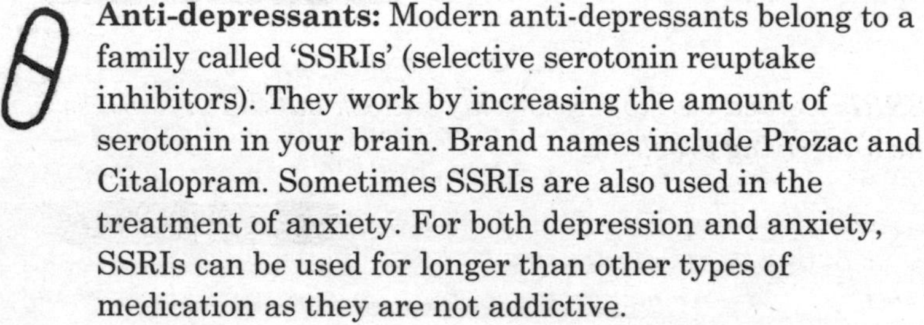

Anti-depressants: Modern anti-depressants belong to a family called 'SSRIs' (selective serotonin reuptake inhibitors). They work by increasing the amount of serotonin in your brain. Brand names include Prozac and Citalopram. Sometimes SSRIs are also used in the treatment of anxiety. For both depression and anxiety, SSRIs can be used for longer than other types of medication as they are not addictive.

Benzodiazepines: You may have heard of Valium (diazepam) or Xanax (alprazolam). These are prescribed in short courses to help with anxiety but can be addictive.

Sleeping tablets: These work in a similar way to benzos. They can only be used in the short term. You may have heard of Zopiclone, Zaleplon and Zolpidem. Over-the-counter treatments, such as Nytol, can also be used in the short term and you should speak to a GP regarding continued use.

Anti-psychotics: This medication (risperidone, arapiprazole) is used to treat people by reducing hallucinations and delusions but it can also reduce the intensity of people's emotions.

Mood stabilisers: Common drugs include lithium. These help level out mood swings.

Over-the-counter remedies: Some people use drugs like St John's wort, 5-HTP or Kalms, which are available without prescription. They are still medication and they can interact with other medications so you should talk to a pharmacist before using these.

'When I was in group CBT I went back to my doctor who then gave me medication as the therapy wasn't working. Once the dosage was sorted out it really did help.'

'SSRIs worked well to improve my outlook but didn't address the underlying problems.'

DR OLIVIA SAYS . . .

Lots of people worry that if they start taking medication, they'll either be on it for the rest of their lives or it will change their personality. This is not going to happen. Medication is generally prescribed in the short term to allow you to access other sources of help and while you learn new coping skills.

There are lots of different medications and lots of different doses. It can take some time to get the balance right. If a person feels their medication is having adverse effects, they should go back to their GP.

Some people do have long-term mental health conditions that are best managed with medication, but even these would be regularly reviewed by a professional and in collaboration with the patient.

The charity Young Minds is the only charity that works exclusively on young people's mental health. On their website *youngminds.org.uk*, there is a phenomenal section about medication and what it might mean in terms of real life – will medication affect your sex drive? Your appetite? There are dozens of case studies to explore too.

SUPPORT IN SCHOOL

For many young people, a trip to the GP may not be necessary when you already have helpful bods at school. Nearly all schools will have a school nurse or a school counsellor (and many secondary schools will have one of these on site).

While these people are unable to provide medication or give the same specialist treatment as a psychiatrist or psychologist, for most of us it wouldn't get that far anyway, so these school-based professionals can be super helpful.

In most cases they will offer a break from lessons, talking therapy and a chance to speak freely with a sympathetic, objective ear.

'We have a school therapist, who has been wonderful, and I've been to see on and off from when I was sixteen. Honestly, talking to friends or family has never been something that has worked for me.'

They cannot promise confidentiality for the reasons I outlined before. And as with any therapist or doctor, if there's a personality clash it probably won't work.

'I'd burst into tears, so [a teacher] made me go talk to a school counsellor, who I felt was so nosy. The counsellor prised me open and got me to tell her everything about my dad's death when I was ten years old. She asked me what I'd brought for lunch that day. I hadn't brought anything, so according to her I had an eating disorder. I remember thinking she must not have a lot to do.'

As well as counsellors and nurses, a good teacher will make time to listen to the issues of their pupils. Again, they are only able to listen and give advice but, vitally, they can offer practical solutions to help you cope with day-to-day life at school. For example, time out from lessons, extended exam time, freedom to go to appointments and longer deadlines.

'The thing that worked best was the support the school gave when they became involved. They often checked up on me, gave me special provisions for exams where I had rest breaks to control my anxiety and deter any panic attacks, and they were very understanding and willing to provide me with extensions for assessments I was having trouble completing due to my mental illness. Knowing that the school cared about my wellbeing was what helped me get out of bed and go to school.'

For some young people, a social worker is another point of contact between them and official channels of support. Social workers can be involved in any child protection concerns.

CHARITIES AND ORGANISATIONS

Charities are wonderful because they produce materials that all young people can easily access in order to help themselves. The Mind website is especially good for this (details in Chapter 13).

For some, a charity's support goes above and beyond literature and they help connect young people with the help they need.

CHAPTER 5

UNDER PRESSURE

COPING WITH STRESS

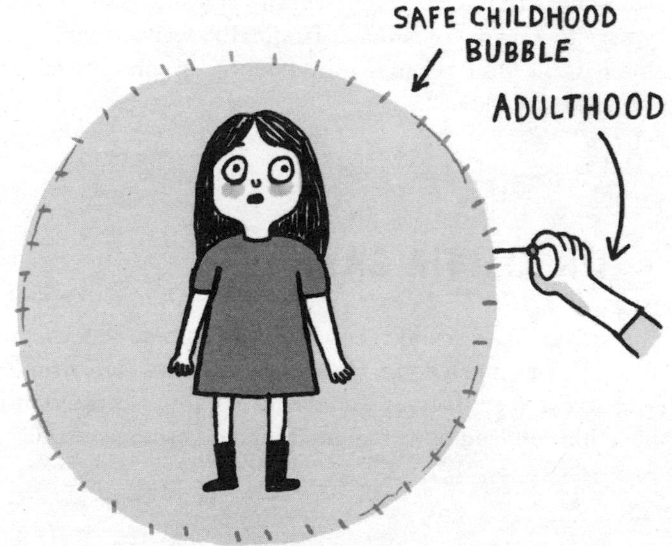

UNDER PRESSURE

Stress is very easy to understand. There's a little formula and everything:

perceived resources – perceived demands = stress level

So! If you think you are equipped to cope with the demands of a situation, you'll be able to handle it. However, if the demands outweigh how good you think you are, you'll start to feel the stress. Maths is fun!

Of course, life events and perceived resources (i.e. how well charged your internal battery is) fluctuate, which means that something that ordinarily wouldn't stress you out might do if you're feeling overwhelmed. Ironically, writing this is stressing me RIGHT OUT because I am about to go on tour with a different book! See?

DR OLIVIA SAYS . . .

Stress is a normal reaction. Without stress, few of us would get very much done. However, when we feel chronically stressed or stressed about lots of things at the same time, this can lead us to feel anxious and out of control.

As Dr Olivia says, a little bit of stress can be a good thing – it gets us out of bed, gets us places on time and makes us push ourselves. Any challenge should come with a little bit of stress, otherwise it's not a challenge, is it? Unless you want to live a very, very limited life, I'm afraid you're going to have to welcome some stress into your world. It isn't pleasant, but nowhere in the small print of life did it say it was going to be pleasant absolutely all the time.

A modified version of the Holmes and Rahe Stress Scale for 'non-adults' lists the most stressful life events as:

1. Death of a parent/sibling
2. Unwanted pregnancy/abortion
3. Getting married (IDEK why non-adults are getting married TBQH)
4. Divorce of parents
5. Acquiring a physical deformity
6. A parent going to jail
7. Peer-group issues
8. Finding out you're adopted
9. Death of a friend
10. Parent remarriage

Each event was assigned a 'life change unit' based on the impact it would have on an individual's life and the likelihood it would lead to illness. These are obviously huge, earth-shattering things (well, with the possible exception of marriage) and it's not surprising to see them top the list. But more surprisingly, only just outside the top ten were academic failure, dating, not being accepted at your first choice university and, perhaps even more surprisingly, academic SUCCESS. It's also worth remembering that, as stress is a highly personal experience, one person's trip to Thorpe Park will be another person's living-fiery-hell dream.

Bottom line is, we're all going to face stressful events – it's our response to them that will vary.

WHAT DOES STRESS LOOK LIKE?

If a person is subjected to a prolonged period of stress, it can manifest in lots of different ways, such as:

BEHAVIOURAL SIGNS[12]	PHYSICAL SIGNS[13]	EMOTIONAL SIGNS[14]	COGNITIVE SIGNS[15]
Eating more or less	Aches and pains	Moodiness	Memory problems
Sleeping too much or too little	Diarrhoea or constipation	Irritability or short temper	Lack of ability to focus
Isolating oneself from others	Increased frequency of urination	Agitation, inability to relax	Poor decision-making
Procrastinating or neglecting responsibilities	Indigestion	Feeling overwhelmed	Negative thoughts
Using alcohol, cigarettes or drugs to relax	Changes in blood glucose	Sense of loneliness and isolation	Restlessness
Nervous habits (e.g. nail biting, pacing)	Nausea	Depression	Regular worrying
	Dizziness	Sadness	
	Chest pain, rapid heartbeat		
	Loss of sex drive		
	Frequent colds		
	Irregular periods		

---

[12] Aldwin, 2007
[13] Seligman, 1990
[14] Seligman, 1975
[15] Carlson & Heth, 2007

DON'T let anybody tell you that, ever. Around puberty, your body – including the chemicals in your head – is in an UNPRECEDENTED state of flux. It's a day-glo rave in your brain and everyone's invited. Furthermore, you are sent to a frenzied daily academic competition that makes *The Hunger Games* look woolly and liberal by comparison. Your teenage years are when your blinkers drop off and you see the world as it really is. The protective bubble provided by your parents often bursts and you find yourself on your own.

It's a stressful time, make no mistake.

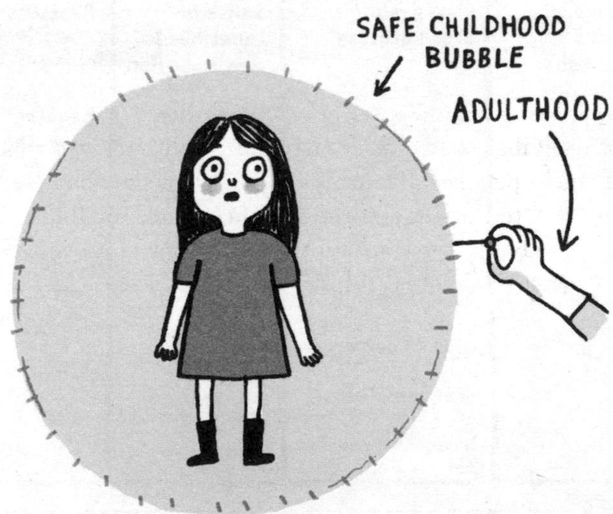

ACADEMIC STRESS

'I experienced periods of severe anxiety while doing my A levels. I felt extremely worried about how I was doing at school. I was conscientious and really cared about my grades but, looking back, the reason I was so anxious was because I was concerned not to let other people down. I felt like I should do well, and that it would look awful if I didn't, which is a lot of pressure. When I had a test coming up I would feel like hiding and be unable to sleep, even getting up and tidying my room at three am to try to get back some control. Sometimes I'd be so anxious about going to a lesson or doing a piece of homework that I thought might not go well, I'd feel nauseous or even be physically sick. I would force myself to go through with them though. I got into trouble with teachers because I couldn't bear to hand in something that might have errors in it, so often "forgot" about deadlines. Unfortunately, I didn't want to ask for help, because I felt doing that would be seen as a failure. I felt completely trapped and helpless.'

As Kate describes, school is a particular nightmare because, by law, all young people must attend – you are somewhat trapped. If you go back to the list of stressful life events, you'll see that it doesn't actually matter whether you're doing well in your subjects or not – school is simply stressful.

I suppose part of the stress is intentional. I'll tell you what else is stressful: work. So a lot of the organisational elements of schooling – deadlines, punctuality, presentation and time-management – are designed to get you ready for the stresses you'll face as an adult. As we've said, stress is part of life; get used to it. But sometimes, if stress is prolonged or gets too great, it can make us feel **WRETCHED**.

Common worries at school are:

- Exam performance
- Academic failure/poor grades
- Letting down parents/teachers
- Not getting into preferred university
- Flunking out and working the till in a pound shop because calculating change in the 99p shop would be too challenging.

Okay, the last one isn't entirely serious, but what all of the above boil down to is the fear we'll limit our future lives if we leave school with less-than-glowing grades.

Well, that's a load of crap. YES, succeeding academically can open doors and offer choices, but they're far from the be-all and end-all. Increasingly, professions and industries are speaking out against factory-line academic success, instead insisting they're looking for verve, personality, creativity and nimble-thinking problem-solvers.

I'd estimate about half of what I've achieved is through good manners, charm and the gift of the gab. I got those skills from my grandma, not from school. Yep, it's all about those 'transferable skills' – politeness, time-keeping, conversation skills and good old-fashioned hard work.

As you well know, exams can be retaken, and universities can be found through the clearing process. Here's a secret no one tells you: so many people have degrees now, there's not much to tell them apart. Where you go and what you study isn't wildly important in many cases.

Speaking from experience, I did my psychology degree because I had NO IDEA what I wanted to do. Why would I? I was seventeen and being asked to make life decisions! What was literally ANYONE thinking when they thought that was a good idea? By the time I was twenty-one, I had decided teaching looked like a fun profession so completed a post-graduate teaching course. THEN, eight years later, I realised that what I actually wanted to do was write stories. There is NO timescale for figuring out what you want to be or do. Take the foot off the accelerator. You have all the time in the world.

'With school grades I considered anything less than an A unacceptable and, despite my parents being nothing but supportive and proud of me, I saw my achievements as "expected" and if anything I did was average, then, in my mind, I had failed.'

What about your parents and teachers? Your parents want you to do well, of course they do, but they also want you to be happy and balanced. If parents knew what putting their children under intense pressure did to them both physically and mentally, every last one would back off. That might mean you need to tell them. Parents are not psychic.

Teachers are the same. Most care deeply about their young wards and want them to reach their full potential. However, be aware that teachers and schools are being judged on their performance. In fact, THEIR pay is now linked to YOUR performance. This is a politically driven system that benefits no one, in which young people have been reduced to numbers and grades. To my mind, politicians, in their desperate attempt to raise standards, may be failing to take into account that young minds can only be pushed so far. Well, hear this: your wellbeing is more important than your grades. Always.

'Perfectionism plays a big part as I attend a prestigious university and have always had above-average grades. But I struggle with tasks like making phone calls and applying for jobs.'

ELLEN 18 DUNDEE

ACADEMIC SUCCESS

TIPS FOR HEALTHY REVISION

- The human brain can only concentrate for twenty minutes or so, so staring at a piece of paper for hours on end isn't going to help you learn anything. Take breaks or switch focus every half an hour.
- Create a sensible timetable for revision well ahead of time. This gives you an opportunity to use some excellent stationery, but also helps you chop the

workload into manageable chunks. Doing two or three half-hour bouts in an evening for three months is far more effective than doing six hours a day for the last week before an exam.

- Try to stick to your exam timetable, but DO NOT feel too bad if things go awry. If you want a night off, take a night off.
- Establish the way you like to revise – try each of these methods until you find one that works for you.
  - ☐ reading
  - ☐ recording notes and playing them back
  - ☐ rewriting notes until they sink in
  - ☐ devising quizzes – get a friend or family member to test you
  - ☐ a combination of these things
- Ensure you eat well, sleep well, take fresh air and exercise.
- NEVER cram the morning of an exam. If you don't know it by then, you're never going to. Go into an exam refreshed, showered and having had a light breakfast.
- After an exam, many people find the 'post-mortem' when answers are compared and dissected with others incredibly stressful. You can't do a THING about your answers then, so just get out of there.

Over the page there is a sensible revision timetable that should get you through even the toughest of exam periods. Scan or photocopy it and add in your subjects.

Note – Saturday doesn't HAVE to be YOUR day off, that's just the day I chose. Each box should represent about thirty minutes of study time – remember, you can't concentrate well for much more than that. On a weekend day or during study leave you could use one of these timetables for mornings and one for afternoons, or divide the cells further.

The breaks are up to you. I'd make a cup of tea and watch ONE episode of *The Powerpuff Girls* back in the day. Whatever your poison, I'd recommend getting up, moving around, possibly getting fresh air and using the loo so you're ready to start again after twenty minutes or so.

Do you really need distractions running in the background? If need be, turn the Wi-Fi router OFF. I know. I went there.

DAY	Week before exams begin	
Monday		BREAK
Tuesday		
Wednesday		
Thursday		
Friday		
Saturday	DAY OFF	
Sunday		

BREAK

FRIENDSHIP ISSUES

*'I have a very rough time with friends who make me feel like I'm not worth anything. It's not a constant issue, but sometimes they make comments like "Your pimple on your cheek looks ready to attack me" or similar, and it makes me feel like sh*t.'*

CHARLOTTE 17 NORWAY

I am in no way surprised that peer-group status features so highly in the stress chart (at number seven). Aside from academic pressures at school, there's a whole bunch of social worries to contend with too. I think a lot of the problem stems from proximity – there are just far too many young people in too small a space. Throw a couple of cameras in any given classroom and you've basically got the Big Brother House.

It's competitive. You're competing for your teacher's attention as well as that of guys or girls. While humans are social creatures, I'm not sure having so many in a such small space ever works well – look at other institutions like prisons – as hierarchies and rivalries inevitably form.

From my time as a teacher, I can tell you these structures are complex, powerful and destructive. For boys, the system is simple: the toughest physically will usually dominate. Bitching and conniving doesn't get boys far – although don't think for a minute that these traits are exclusively female. Girls' friendship groups tend to be more complex, from my experience. Instead of physical strength, it's more a social war of wills, in which pawns are won over to opposing sides, or boys and items are traded. Girls in particular may find their social stock rising or plummeting and this can make life very stressful indeed.

Calling such problems 'friendship issues' cruelly trivialises a huge cause of stress. During adolescence, as we slightly 'phase out' the importance of our family, our friends and relationships take on a huge significance.

'I spent a year abroad and when I came back started at a new school. Things had shifted with my old friends and I hadn't yet really made new friends. I felt quite isolated but it was more than that – I got irrationally upset when plans fell through or if people were busy. I kind of knew it was irrational but it didn't stop this build-up of frustration, anger and loneliness. I'd end up sitting and crying for hours, I remember desperately wanting to throw stuff just to vent the frustration, and when I wasn't doing that I was usually asleep, hiding from it.'

HANNAH LONDON

There is no easy answer for remedying peer-group issues or the stress they cause. I do think this though: humans can never BELONG to other humans, and very often OWNERSHIP of friends seems to be an issue – 'You're MY friend, not HERS!', that sort of thing.

Friends come and go. Not a popular topic of any film or book you've ever seen, but the cold, hard truth. Some friendships are toxic to poisonous levels, and no friend is worth damaging your health over. Here's another truth: you'll make new friends. Honestly! You will! As people change and evolve, you look for people with similar interests and outlooks. Over your teens and into your twenties, people will inevitably come and go, and that, as they say, is life.

So don't be afraid to opt out of a damaging friendship group. The only person you can control is you. Be fun, be friendly and, most importantly, be KIND. Do that and you'll be a brilliant friend who attracts other NEW, fun, friendly, kind people. Don't let toxicity infect you. That's ALL you can do.

BULLYING

The stereotype of the shaven-headed meat-fiend jumping out from a smoky toilet stall to flush your head down the loo is something of a myth. Most bullying issues tend to form within friendships (see above). This can make bullying situations very complex, with shots being fired from all sides. On any given day an individual can be both victim and perpetrator when it comes to verbal or physical aggression, poop-stirring and gossip-trading.

I speak from experience. I was both. School was hell.

Many students and parents still have the wrong idea about how teachers and schools define bullying.

BULLYING IS . . . THE THREE Ps:

Purposeful: There is intent. Accidents happen; it doesn't make them bullying.

Persistent: It happens time and time again. Sometimes people lash out – verbally or physically. If this happens, it should be reported as an incident and you should tell someone, but it isn't bullying. However, if the same person is always being singled out, it almost certainly is victimisation.

Powerful: There's a power imbalance in the relationship. It's very hard for an individual to 'bully' a group. It's similarly difficult (although not impossible) for a Year 8 student to bully a Year 13 one. Imagine, however, a group of Year 8s bullying a painfully shy Year 13 girl about her weight. The power has shifted and it IS bullying.

If you think you ARE being victimised, you don't have to be a victim. Take action – you've done nothing wrong. While it's very easy for me to say 'tell someone', I stress that I went down the 'I hope it'll go away if I keep quiet' route and, you know what? It didn't. By staying silent, you give the other party all the power – you are complicit in the 'it'll be our little secret' mentality. By telling someone – especially an authority figure, although even a friend could provide help – you pull power away from them.

I think the most important thing is to collect evidence. Remember how we said bullying has to be persistent? So get your facts straight with this handy form, which can be photocopied or scanned.

Date:
Location:
Who was involved?
What happened?
What did you do?
Who else saw it happen?

Take your completed forms to a teacher or school counsellor. They'll find such evidence very hard to ignore. Also, it'll help you keep events straight in your mind.

BOYFRIENDS AND GIRLFRIENDS

Dating and breaking up also feature pretty highly on the life-events stress scale. It's odd to me that something that's supposed to bring joy to people can cause so much heartache, but heartbreak there is. Unrequited love is bad enough but even if you DO get someone interested, the path to true love can be fraught. Whether you're in the early, middle or later stages of a relationship, there are stresses and strains at every turn.

In the early days, much sleep is lost while trying to figure out if someone likes you back or whether you really like them. This is a perfectly normal part of the dating process. Common symptoms include anxiously waiting for responses to text messages and reading hidden meanings in emojis.

I'd hazard that if you're finding it excessively stressful, it might not be the relationship for you. Here's the thing: when it's right, it's right. Shakespeare may well have said 'the course of true love never did run smooth' but he was a touch histrionic. Actually, there doesn't and shouldn't need to be a three-act drama if it's the right relationship.

When you've been together a while, an abundance of stress is a key indicator that it might be time to move on. Are you:

- going through each other's phones/inboxes?
- fretting your partner is up to no good?

- checking up on them constantly?
- bickering, arguing and fighting?
- verbally or physically abusing one another?

An unhealthy relationship is going to cause stress that will impact on your overall health. No relationship is worth sacrificing your health for. Ever.

The end of a relationship, whether you're the one being dumped or doing the dumping, can be hugely traumatic and is very much a loss. We'll examine this more in chapter 7.

SEX

Sex can be a huge cause of stress. No one, no matter how much porn-time they've logged online, is born a sexpert, and whether you're a beginner or an intermediate, sex can always be nerve-wracking. In fact, porn is probably a sure-fire way to fill your head with misconceptions about sex.

Worrying about sex is quite normal for all young people. It's a paradox: too little sex is stressful *(why doesn't anyone want me?)*; too much sex is stressful *(what will everyone think?).* You'll note that only one of these worries applies to men.

Hopefully your school has or had a rigorous sex education syllabus that has answered all the questions you may have about sex. Hopefully you feel happy and confident about your body (there will be more on body issues in chapter 8). Hopefully you understand that consensual sex is a healthy part of a relationship if both partners want it. Hopefully you understand that both males and females are allowed to have as much consensual sex as they like without fear of judgement. Hopefully you know that sex is nothing like you've seen in porn.

Understanding all these things should lead to some pretty stress-free sex. If all the minutes people spent needlessly worrying about sex were to be harvested as an energy source, we could all stop drilling for oil and gas tomorrow.

'When I was fourteen, I went to my first party, and had my first taste of alcohol. I ended up getting "blackout drunk", and hooking up with an older guy. I had a boyfriend at the time. The whole school found out, and people I'd never met before were yelling "SLUT!" at me as I walked to class. At first I kept insisting that the people who really knew me knew I wasn't "like that", so I didn't care what others said, but eventually I gave in, and started calling myself a slut.'

Clearly, that's not cool. Don't ever use words like 'slut', 'slag', 'whore', 'ho' or 'slapper' – whoever you're talking about, they're deeply gendered, and mostly say to me you're jealous you're not having more snogs.

LGBTQ*

'I was bullied [and unable] to accept my sexuality, mainly because I didn't really understand it and didn't know anyone I felt I could or wanted to talk about these issues with.'

For about 5% of all the young people in the world, there is an additional stress to the usual dating strains. Don't get me wrong, being lesbian, gay, bisexual, queer or transgender is not an automatic source of stress. For many people, figuring their identity can be an enlightening process of self-discovery.

For others, the process of identification and coming out can be enormously stressful. For one thing, many young LGBT* people will have to carry a secret around with them for a good while and this is stressful in itself. Lying to cover one's tracks is exhausting.

Straight and cisgender (not trans) people will never have to worry about parents reacting badly to coming out. They'll never have to worry about being thrown onto the streets because of their sexuality or true gender. They'll never have to worry about homophobic abuse. These ARE valid concerns, but they're extraordinarily rare. Yes, some parents need time to deal with a child's sexuality, but nearly ALL get over it sooner rather than later.

What makes me very sad are statistics that show the prevalence of mental health issues among young lesbian, gay, bisexual, transgender, queer and curious people. A 2014 survey by LGBTQ* support group METRO found that 42% of young LGBTQ* people sought medical help for depression or anxiety, compared with 29% of straight, cisgendered youths; 52% had self-harmed (compared with 35%) and 44% had considered suicide compared with 26% of heterosexual, non-trans respondents. Other studies have also reported a marked contrast in substance abuse, homelessness and risky sexual behaviour for young LGBTQ* people.

All I can think is that these stats reflect the added FEAR young LGBTQ* people have to face. We're still decades away from the sort of societal acceptance some people think we already have. LGBTQ* people still get to experience fear of rejection, abandonment and isolation. I'd like nothing more than to be able to say to you right now that no LGBTQ* youngsters are rejected by their loved ones because we're not in 1958 any more, but it does still happen.

However, it doesn't happen very often, or when it does families are usually able to work through their issues given time and support. The FEAR is often worse than the reality (isn't that always the way?) but once fear starts making young people want to self-harm or take their lives it becomes oh-so-real.

Listen. Every magnificent LGBTQ* adult was once a kid learning to live with the FEAR. It reaches peak scariness right before you come out and then, slowly, gets a little bit better every day after. Doesn't mean it's easy, doesn't mean there won't be mental health issues waiting for you on the other side, because literally no one gets that free pass – but DO hang in there. One day you'll wonder what you were so scared of, I promise.

DR OLIVIA SAYS . . .

It may be that talking through a stressful situation with someone can help give you a different perspective or provide some ideas for coping. Other strategies include writing down all the things that are stressing you out. Is there anything you can do about these things? If not, then stressing about them probably won't help either. Otherwise, think of one small thing that will make a difference and write it down. At the end you should have a list of small things that you can do to manage your stress.

It might also be helpful to look at other areas of your life. Exercise, sleep and diet all interact with your overall stress levels.

I helpfully wrote an entire book about the concerns surrounding coming out. It's called *This Book Is Gay* and it will help. But as you're holding this book now, I shall assure you that coming out is the best way to reduce a lot of stress – but may also lead to new ones once you start dating! For many, 'coming out' is a bit like ripping off a plaster: painful, but over quite quickly.

Rest assured that stresses surrounding your identity are temporary and will, as the saying goes, get better.

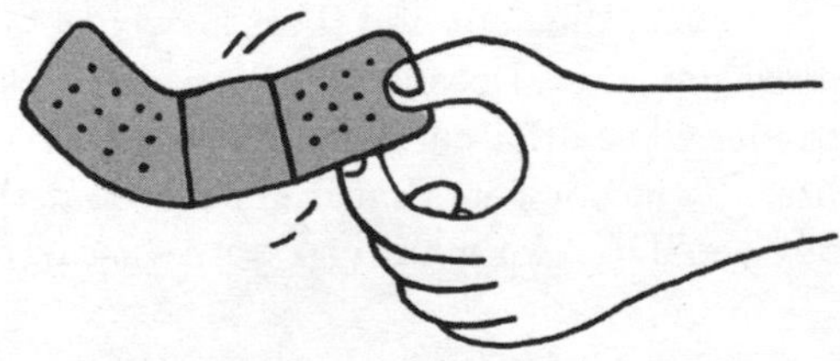

CHAPTER 6

BEYOND WORRY

ABOUT ANXIETY

BEYOND WORRY

Worry, whether we like it or not (clue: NO ONE LIKES WORRY), is part of being human. Driving lessons, getting to an airport on time, going on a date, that bit just before an exam – if these things AREN'T making you feel nervous, I'd love to know how you do it.

I hope it brings some comfort to know that EVERYONE is feeling like they might genuinely die just before their driving test. TALK ABOUT IT. Saying 'Holy cow, I really might vom, that Pop-Tart was a HUGE mistake' is the best way to let some air out of its tyres. Laughter IS the best medicine (after SSRIs, obv).

But Anxiety (capital A, not just regular old 'worry') is increasingly common among young people. Along with depression, it's by far the most frequently reported mental health complaint. But we must be clear: being worried about exams or making friends is NOT anxiety. Right now, anxiety is quite trendy, although I cannot fathom why. Given my own hideous anxiety attacks, I assure you it's something I wouldn't wish on my worst enemy.

We all worry, we will all experience a degree of 'little a' anxiety, but at what stage does WORRY become CAPITAL A ANXIETY?

DR OLIVIA SAYS . . .

Anxiety is the anticipation of fear. People can get anxious about all sorts of situations, thoughts or external things – dogs or spiders, even.

While being anxious about things is normal for everyone – who wouldn't be nervous before an exam? – when anxiety becomes severe or carries on for a long time, it can start impacting on daily life, and this is when it becomes a problem.

When we feel anxious, it is because our body is releasing a hormone called adrenaline. It does this because it perceives a threat. This is so our body is ready to either get the hell out of a perilous situation or find the strength to open a can of whoop-ass. This is commonly known as the 'fight or flight' response. However, given that most of us aren't Buffy the Vampire Slayer, we don't really need EXCESS adrenaline. It stays in our system and makes us feel frankly bizarre unless we know how to manage it.

The 'FIGHT OR FLIGHT' RESPONSE

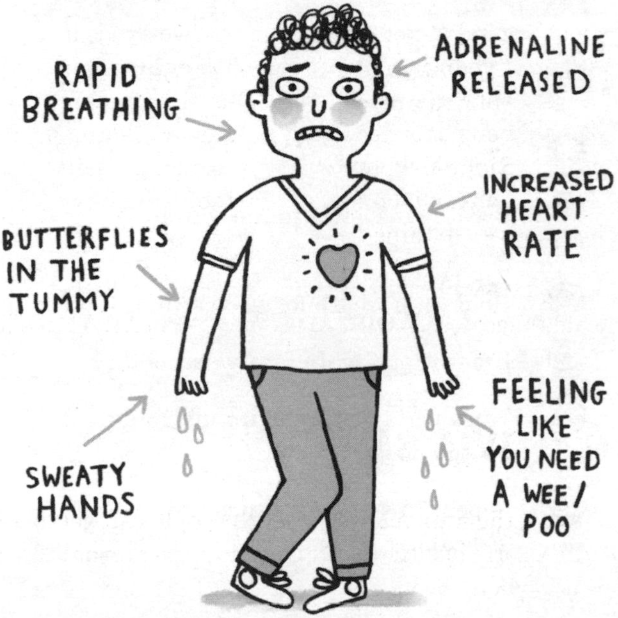

The physical effects of adrenaline include: increased heart rate, rapid breathing, sweaty hands, butterflies in the tummy and feeling like we need an emergency wee or poo.

'Throughout secondary school I would feel nauseous, faint and nervous before school.'

There are numerous effective tricks we can ALL use to reduce anxiety. They are all similar in that they share the goal of making a person more able to diffuse an anxious situation. You can find advice online or in therapy but here's one simple trick:

TRY THIS:

- Lie down and put your hands on your tummy.
- Close your eyes.
- Breathe in slowly to the count of five.
- Hold your breath for two seconds.
- Breathe out again for five seconds.
- You should feel your tummy going up and down.
- Repeat this several times until you feel calmer.

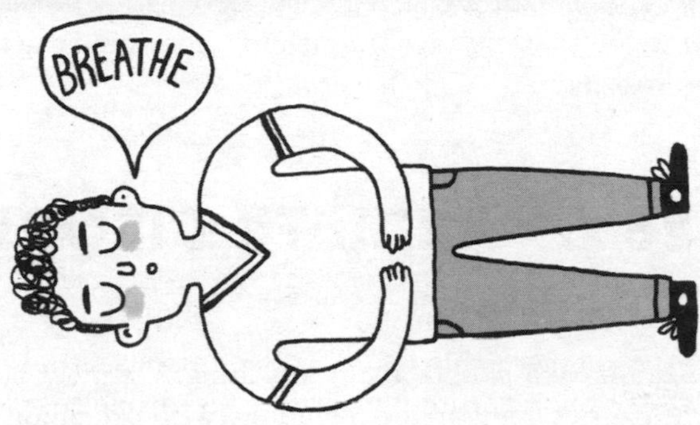

How did that feel? Focusing all your energy on something as simple as breathing enables you to clear your mind to avoid escalating the anxiety. As anxiety is the fear of fear, distracting the mind is a good plan. Slowing your breathing has a PHYSICAL effect on the body and rebalances the oxygen levels in your blood. The excess adrenaline is dispersed and you are fine again.

DR OLIVIA SAYS . . .

Given that anxiety leads to people avoiding things that cause undue worry, a common treatment for [diagnosed] anxiety disorder is to expose the sufferer to the things that scare them. This is done very gradually and only after a range of coping strategies have been taught. This means a sufferer can face their fear, and are able to control their response.

This is usually done through a regime of CBT with a professional – again using the therapy's techniques to undermine the negative thought patterns.

TYPES OF ANXIETY DISORDER

SPECIFIC PHOBIAS

A person can have a phobia about anything. We must be careful not to confuse 'not being a fan of spiders' with arachnophobia. A true phobia is crippling and can massively impact on a person's life.

'For as long as I can remember I had an "issue" with illness; I was utterly petrified of getting sick, seeing sick, being sick. I thought that all of the worry and panic – sweaty palms, irrational thoughts, headaches, shoulder and neck pain from being so tense – I thought all of this was normal, until it caused me to put myself in danger at work. It was then that I knew I couldn't go on just pretending everything was okay.

It started with little things: if my younger sister was sick, I couldn't stay in the room to help out. Then I couldn't watch it on TV, or see drawings or cartoons of illness or sick. I started washing my hands – a lot. I would sniff and feel mugs and glasses repeatedly to see if they smelt and felt clean. I held my breath as I walked down the corridor past the nurse's office to avoid inhaling germs – even if there was nobody around who was unwell – and I would do the same while walking through large crowds or near a group of people. I stopped drinking on nights out, and would often have to leave a nightclub or pub for fear that someone was going to spontaneously erupt in a volcanic explosion of beer-spew. I couldn't eat restaurant chicken, and if we were eating it at home I had to cook it myself or watch the other person cook it and thoroughly wash all utensils after use. I wouldn't use canteen cutlery and brought my own disposables. I survived like this – and steadily got worse – for probably twelve years before my fear and coping behaviours put me in danger and I had to do something about it.'

SOCIAL ANXIETY DISORDER

Does what is says on the tin. Sufferers will start to dread certain social situations. This isn't 'being a bit shy around new people', although that could be the start of it for some sufferers. Often a negative experience can be the root of worry, which turns to dread, which turns to anxiety.

'When I was eighteen, I had a serious case of social anxiety that was undiagnosed and caused me to have severe panic attacks while at college to the point where I could no longer even think about going to college – or the town it was in – without my hands/arms shaking and feeling ill.'

My issues are actually a type of social anxiety disorder. Can I present to 500 readers at a convention? Yes! Do I love going on tour? Yes! Do I have a crippling fear of needing to go to the loo on public transport? Also yes. You can see how it happened, really, can't you? Having IBS attacks while pottering around London over the last few years has developed into a more serious issue. I stress I've never ACTUALLY pooped myself – I'd tell you if I had – but just worrying I MIGHT and that people would JUDGE is enough to send me into blind panic, which leads us nicely to . . .

PANIC DISORDER

People are very quick to say they're having a panic attack if they're a little bit warm or suspect they've left an oven on. But what is an ACTUAL panic attack all about?

DR OLIVIA SAYS . . .

Panic attacks come on very suddenly, are hugely intense and are mostly located in your body. By this I mean it's not so much anxious thoughts or worries as it is physical sensations, such as heart palpitations, sweating, trembling, shortness of breath, chest pains. It feels like there is something physically wrong so people often think they're having a heart attack or a nervous breakdown.

Panic attacks and anxiety are closely linked. Sometimes panic attacks can lead to anxiety because a sufferer starts to worry about having panic attacks (thus making a panic attack more likely), while some people have panic attacks as a result of existing anxieties. The onset of a panic attack can start a downward spiral of physical symptoms – shallow, rapid breathing can actually increase heart rate, making a sufferer feel worse. This is why immediate intervention for a panic attack will often feature breathing exercises, such as breathing into a paper bag. NEVER use a plastic bag and watch out for inhaling receipts!

AGORAPHOBIA

This is the perception of certain places being dangerous – sometimes (but not always) wide open spaces. This isn't necessarily, as often portrayed on TV, a fear of going outside.

GENERALISED ANXIETY DISORDER

Anxiety has a nasty habit of becoming generalised. What may start out as a specific phobia can develop into worries about lots of other unrelated things.

OBSESSIVE COMPULSIVE DISORDER

Beyond light switches and bleach – what is obsessive compulsive disorder (OCD) really about?

DR OLIVIA SAYS . . .

We can all understand how we get anxious about things in the world, but what happens when we get anxious about thoughts in our head? Most people have strange or illogical thoughts. Normally we notice them and dismiss them as irrelevant. However, people with OCD notice these intrusive thoughts and feel compelled to do something about them.

Try this exercise. Fill the blank in this sentence:

Tonight, I hope

____

(insert name of loved one)
is involved in a fatal car accident.

Be honest – were you able to do that? It's not easy is it? Even though we know that writing a name in a gap doesn't make something any more likely to happen, it's still difficult. We call these types of thoughts 'MAGICAL THINKING'. It's a developmental stage most of us go through as children.

Some people with OCD get stuck on trying to neutralise these kinds of thoughts. The form these neutralising thoughts or actions take will vary dramatically from person to person. It could be something in the sufferer's head, like counting, or a physical action, such as checking. These compulsions are incredibly difficult to resist and can have a huge impact on day-to-day life.

OCD IS NOT:

- a cleaning disorder
- checking the doors are locked
- germ phobia
- having a neat workspace or sharpened pencils
- being picky about food

For some people, the compulsions MAY take all or some of these actions, along with an infinite number more. Nevertheless, bandying around phrases like 'OMG LOL, I'M WELL OCD ABOUT MY DUVET! LOL!' is deeply insensitive to actual sufferers.

SAM'S STORY

Sam, 18, from Kent, struggled with OCD when he was younger.

'I used to repeat sentences. I'd say something out loud, everyone would hear and I don't know why but I'd just have to say it again. I've always repeated things; I think that's something that will never go away. There's a worry that I've not quite said what I meant to say or there's more that could be said. It can be really annoying.

It was at the start of secondary school when it got noticeable. When I was young it didn't bother me, but the older I got the more I knew that it wasn't quite normal, so it became more frustrating and I think the frustration made it a lot worse.

I had loads of strange habits, set routines that I couldn't break. One was washing my hands. Another was when I woke up I had to do a certain stretch and if I didn't do that stretch I'd be angry for the rest of the day, like furious at myself. My worst one was I'd check things on the floor, so I'd walk past something and see it in the corner of my eye, and I'd have to go back and check what it was. Once I walked back a good couple of hundred metres because I'd seen something and I couldn't let it go. It was really weird and that was the one my mum was most concerned about.

I used to get really bad migraines at least three or four times a week because of the stress and the tension and repeating stuff.

There are so many misconceptions. That's something I struggle with; lots of other people didn't understand. I got in a lot of trouble at school mainly because I was angry all the time and struggling to deal with it – I didn't deal with it well. One year I got excluded about thirty times. It was very hard because not only did I not understand what was happening, I knew that everyone else around me didn't either because the advice they gave just wasn't helpful or useful.

I had depression at the time as well so Mum and me kept going back to the GP. There was one GP, it wasn't my regular one, who suggested healthy living rather than issuing the medication. I had to go and see a specialist who said, "Yeah, put him on Prozac," so Mum realised just how serious it was. I think Mum was frustrated she couldn't do more or know more about it but she definitely helped a lot. I spoke to a psychiatrist who was the first person I'd spoken to who did understand.

The medication helped slightly but obviously there were side effects. It made me really hungry. I ate a lot and I got quite chubby. I couldn't play football very well any more (I was never that good in the first place!).

I also started to get some therapy, which was really helpful. There were certain techniques the therapist told me about that took some getting used to but I still use them now.

I decided to come off the medication. I didn't want to be on medication all my life. It had to be done gradually but eventually I got rid of it and it was the techniques from therapy that kept me going. It was tough, but after a few weeks school started getting better. I had a really good summer because it was the first time I could go outside.

I drink a lot. Once I start drinking, I drink a lot because, for me, the OCD voice switches off, which is maybe why I like it so much. Obviously when I'm that drunk I can get into a lot of trouble. I wouldn't say I'm addicted. If I was told to stop by a doctor I could and I would stop drinking. But for the moment I enjoy doing it because it numbs the OCD and I feel good when I drink. So I'm going to carry on doing it. I don't know whether that would count as self-medication. I've never drunk because of OCD. The main thing is I can easily see how and why people would self-medicate with alcohol.

Personally I'd say you've got to come to terms with the fact that this is something you're going to have to deal with, most likely, for the rest of your life. For me it was a long process. It was about accepting what I couldn't change, but changing what I couldn't accept. There's a lot of small things that I do, like double-locking the car. That takes five seconds of my time. I know it's my OCD but it doesn't impact me that much. But walking a hundred metres up a road and turning round and running back to look at a stick is not acceptable – can't do that, got to change it, got to fight it, got to beat it. I'll never be able to cut it out altogether, but it's about fighting it to a realistic extent I suppose.'

CHAPTER 7

FEELING BLUE

DEPRESSION – WITH A BIG D AND A LITTLE D

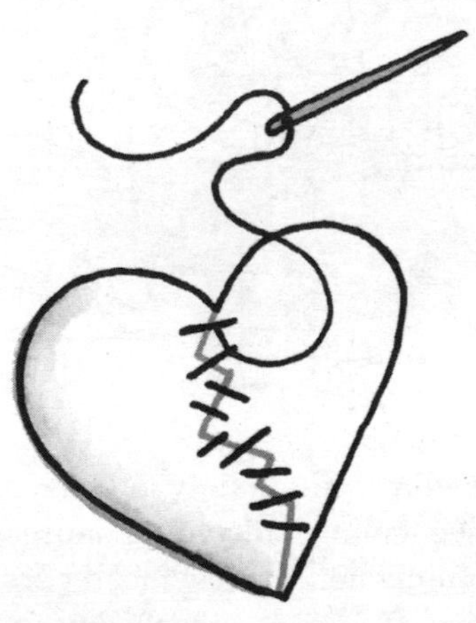

FEELING BLUE

Malaise, melancholy, the blues, low-spiritedness, mournfulness, sorrow, dolefulness, misery, desolation, broken-heartedness. So many words for the same feeling. Why so many? Because, for writers, there's something almost seductive about sadness, something almost appealing about wallowing in despair.

Without sadness, we wouldn't appreciate happiness, and no one (except cabin crew) can be happy all the time. This means there will be downswings in everyone's mood from time to time. We might say 'I'm feeling a bit depressed', and that's fine, but do be aware there is a clear difference between small d and BIG D depression (also known as 'clinical depression') as we shall see later.

As we discussed before with anxiety and stress, we will all experience negative feelings, including depressed spells. The turning point is often when the low mood persists for a length of time and/or starts to impact on your day-to-day routine.

We should view low mood on a scale:

And everything in between. As with all illness perceptions, one person's 'a bit sad' is another's 'depressed'. There is no definitive way for me to tell if you're currently experiencing low mood or clinical depression.

What are the warning signs of depression? What should we be looking out for? The tell-tale tracks are very similar to those of stress. This makes perfect sense as stress can alter your mood to a depressed state.

So be alert to when you:

- can't sleep or sleep too much
- can't concentrate or find that previously easy tasks are now difficult
- feel hopeless and helpless
- dwell on negative thoughts
- have lost your appetite or you can't stop eating
- are much more irritable, short-tempered or aggressive than usual

 are consuming more alcohol than normal or engaging in other reckless behaviour

 have thoughts that life is not worth living (seek help immediately if this is the case).

Temporarily, some or all of these symptoms are bound to catch up with us just through the daily grind. But some life events are traumatic and do impact hugely on our mental health. Before we look at clinical depression, let's examine some life events that are likely to take their toll.

DIVORCE

'From the age of 11 to 14, my parents were undergoing a prolonged, tortuous and damaging divorce. My dad was drinking heavily and used to disappear for days; my mum was angry and eventually took me and my brother out of the family home. I cried myself to sleep each night, and never truly forgave my parents.'

In the UK in 2012 42% of marriages ended in divorce so the chances that your parents or carers might separate aren't too unrealistic. For thousands and thousands of young people, parental divorce is a reality.

We can tell ourselves that relationships don't always work out and that people grow apart over time, but it's still hard to shake that feeling of abandonment if a parent moves out.

Many young people take it personally and such thinking can lead to a very low mood and many of the symptoms listed above.

Remember that, very often, when parents decide to split it's because they have YOU in mind. No one wants a home environment to be fraught with arguments, so a parent leaving is in the hope of creating peace and harmony.

Also bear in mind – and I mean this in the nicest possible way – this isn't about you. As much as we like to think we are the centre of our parents' universe (and we kind of are in many respects), they need to have an adult life with adult relationships too. Not all of these relationships work out. As we mature ourselves, we start to understand that people cannot act purely to please us and must also do what is best for them. That said, even if you're old enough to recognise this fact, it doesn't necessarily make it any less painful or stressful. Whatever age you are when your parents divorce, it's usually a big, unwelcome change. No one likes those.

The good news is it's likely a number of your friends will have already experienced divorce. How did they get through it? You'll have seen that it can be a turbulent time, but one that almost always levels out.

A final piece of advice would be to STAY OUT OF IT. This is your parents' issue to solve, not yours. Don't get caught in the crossfire.

If you're finding your parents hard work (and it doesn't have to be because they're getting divorced), make a list of other adults you could track down for advice or a shoulder to cry on. Is there a school counsellor, teacher or other relative you feel you could turn to?

1. ....

2. ....

3. ....

BREAK-UPS

Like divorce, the end of your own relationships can very much feel like a loss. The dynamics of a love split depend on which side of the split you were on – were you the dumper or the dumpee?

As the dumper, you'll experience feelings of guilt. Guilt is tough, but it's tougher to be on the dumpee end. Although it feels AWFUL knowing you've hurt someone, at least as the dumper you've had time to process what's about to happen and you've chosen to do so as you're planning a positive change. That's not to say this time won't be sad and stressful because it absolutely will be.

The most important thing to remember as a dumper is to BE KIND. Always break up with someone face-to-face. Doing it any other way will only cause you trouble further down the line. Explain to your partner in as much detail as you can why you no longer want to be with them. Don't shift the blame – if you want to leave them, it's YOUR CHOICE; you have to explain. Once it's done, continue to hear them out, reply to calls and texts and, if necessary, reiterate your reasons for wanting to end the relationship.

It's perhaps harder to be the one getting dumped as it comes with both surprise and rejection. No one likes rejection. It can be a real downward spiral: what did I do wrong? Was it something I said? Why aren't I good enough? And so forth.

Understand that it's not YOU that's at fault: the issue is in the COMBINATION. Some combinations work, others don't. The bottom line is, you can only ever be you. You can't change to suit someone else. Just because it didn't work out with one person, doesn't mean it won't with another.

The emotions a person goes through when breaking up with someone are very much those involved with loss, and the stress can manifest in any combination of those listed above. But understand that while we might always have a little scar on our heart, we do heal with time. Being sad is quite boring, after all, and there's only so long you can pine before they just start to annoy you from afar.

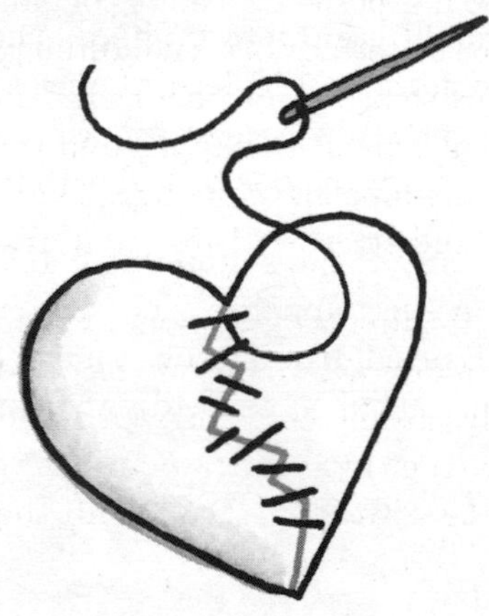

Seeing an ex with a new partner ALWAYS stings though, believe me.

So yes, being dumped or dumping someone WILL feel awful, but the awfulness will, in the vast majority of cases, be temporary.

BEREAVEMENT

DR OLIVIA SAYS . . .

Bereavement can have a lot of the same symptoms as depression. However, bereavement is a normal grief reaction that will resolve itself over time. As mental health professionals, we wouldn't treat someone for DEPRESSION until at least six months after a death, although we might prescribe a short course of sleeping pills or anti-depressants to enable bereaved people to cope.

The loss of a loved one is traumatic for everyone, but grief can manifest in myriad different ways. There is no right or wrong way to grieve. I sometimes wonder if the pressure to cry, sob, sniff and mourn a certain way is as stressful as the loss itself. When someone dies, everyone has to deal with it in their own way.

Grief can look like any of the symptoms listed at the start of this chapter – it can affect appetite, sleep patterns and attention span AS WELL AS mood. It might even mean going into denial for a spell. It doesn't mean someone doesn't care.

With death, break-ups and divorce what we're really dealing with is LOSS, and death is the most permanent loss of all. It's someone we love who is not coming back. That sucks. Sometimes that realisation can take time.

But death is the last chapter for everyone. We know this. The hard part is the reality of missing someone and wishing they were still here – the yearning is awful, but it does ease off. Yes, you'll miss a person, maybe for ever, but after a while it becomes more of a glow than an ache. You simply remember them fondly. A lot of people find comfort in visiting a grave or a monument and talking to a passed love one – and if it makes you feel better, why not?

Be assured that the person who has gone is now at rest and would want you to be at peace too.

NOW – just because grief or relationships issues don't count as big D Depression doesn't mean you shouldn't address any mental health symptoms you might be experiencing. After all, a sustained period of sleeplessness is going to soon develop into more serious issues. Therefore there is no shame at all in asking for help, even for acute issues. A short course of sleeping pills or SSRIs are often prescribed to get sufferers through a tough time. Remember, taken properly they are not addictive and can prevent a turbulent spell becoming chronic illness.

CLINICAL DEPRESSION

DR OLIVIA SAYS . . .

Clinical depression is characterised by changes in mood, thought processes and behaviour. Key criteria for distinguishing between 'low mood' and clinical depression are how long it lasts for and the impact it has on your daily life.

So we've established that we're all going to be sad from time to time, especially if we experience loss. But when does 'sad' become small-d depressed and when does that become Big D Depression?

Well, the word 'depressed' is a word like any other. You can depress a button just as your state can be depressed. I think clinical depression is something else. As Dr Olivia pointed out, it's all about the duration of the depressed state.

Because scientists believe depression and low mood in general are caused by low levels of the brain chemical serotonin, the depressive symptoms will continue until the imbalance is corrected, changing your behaviour, even your sleeping and eating, as well as your thought patterns.

People with depression can become stuck in negative thought patterns. This is not them being wilfully gloomy or emo, it's simply a result of those pesky brain chemicals.

This type of thinking is 'ruminative thinking' and goes something like this:

I AM NOT GOOD ENOUGH

I WISH I WAS BETTER AT THINGS

OTHER PEOPLE ARE BETTER AT THINGS

WHY CAN'T I BE BETTER?

I AM THE WORST AT STUFF

EVERYONE ELSE IS BETTER THAN ME

I BET THEY'RE BETTER THAN ME

THEY'RE BETTER AT THAT TOO

I'M THE WORST AT EVERYTHING

EVEN THAT STRANGER IS BETTER THAN ME

I CAN'T TRY ANY HARDER

NO ONE ELSE EVEN HAS TO TRY

EVEN IF I TRY IT'S NOT GOOD ENOUGH

I AM NOT GOOD ENOUGH

And on and on . . .

If that was hard to read, imagine what it's like in your head ALL THE TIME. As you can imagine, a sustained period of that kind of thinking would grind anyone down. A person having the same thoughts over and over very quickly starts to believe such ruminative thoughts, however odd they seem to a healthy person.

It's like a novelty pop song – even the most awful one can lodge itself in your head and, before you know it, you've learned the words.

'I stopped sleeping, lost all interest in hobbies, even football, which was my passion. I was plagued by obsessive thoughts, particularly about what people saw in me and whether they liked me. I often felt abandoned and alone and would just stay in bed and try to hide from the world. On a few occasions I scratched myself when I became frustrated and angry and didn't know how else to deal with the emotions and thoughts in my head.'

The worst thing about depression is that it squeezes the enjoyment out of the things and people you used to love. It leeches your motivation until even the easiest of things are a mammoth undertaking. Ironically, one thing that WILL help a sufferer feel better is DOING THINGS. Even when people are depressed, if they are asked to do something, they often report they enjoyed it more than anticipated, and that activity lifted their mood.

Basically, anything is better than wallowing in your pyjamas and watching Jeremy Kyle. THAT helps no one.

'I would have periods of feeling utterly lost and I couldn't see the point of anything. I didn't want to go to school, I felt like none of my friends could really stand me, and I felt like I didn't enjoy anything any more. I had very little appetite at most times, and I constantly felt guilty about that because it worried my parents. Even then, I felt invisible and unimportant.'

Remember, depression is an ILLNESS. Although scientists are still learning what brings about changes in people's brains during depression, they do know that sufferers often have low levels of serotonin. However, there is much debate over cause and effect – which came first, the depression or the low levels of serotonin?

SSRIs work for lots of people (although not everyone) so we can assume serotonin is an important factor in some way.

DR OLIVIA SAYS . . .

Medication can be helpful both as a treatment in itself, but also in allowing people to have enough energy and motivation to undergo therapy or other non-medical treatments.

People worry about becoming 'zombie-like' or addicted to anti-depressants. These medications are not addictive and definitely won't turn anyone into a zombie. This may have been true of old-fashioned medications, but newer treatments are unlikely to have these side effects.

In very, very, VERY extreme cases, people can be prescribed electroconvulsive therapy (ECT). Electric currents are put through the brain, and it can help when people are severely depressed and nothing else has worked. I wouldn't worry too much about this tbh.

As clinical depression is an illness, I think it would be dangerous of me to suggest nothing but a bit of exercise and activity will make you all better. A bit of fresh air wouldn't cure a cracked rib and it won't make depression magically disappear either.

If you have experienced a very low mood for a sustained period, it's time to seek help. You can and will get better with the right support, but that all-important first step has to come from you. Remember everything we said in chapter 4 – the right support for you may not be the first doctor or counsellor you see, but don't give up. This is a health issue that shouldn't go unchecked.

LOUISE'S STORY

'In my second year at university in London (aged eighteen) I suffered my first depressive episode. It was severe enough to keep me locked in my room in my shared college flat.

I couldn't get out of bed, couldn't eat – I certainly couldn't carry on with my coursework. I slept for maybe eighteen or nineteen hours a day and I was always tired. I felt utterly numb and alone.

At first I didn't know what was wrong with me: I thought it was flu – my whole body hurt, but I wouldn't take painkillers because, in a funny way, I was glad I could feel something.

I'd been feeling disconnected for a while, and this was something new. I thought it meant I was getting better. Over the course of a couple of weeks, I actually got worse and withdrew further and further.

I was paranoid, convinced that people were talking about me wherever I went, and this made me feel more and more isolated. I considered suicide – passively at first: ideas like allowing myself to fall in front of a Tube, or stepping in front of a bus. The thoughts became more and more intrusive until one day I found myself standing at the edge of the Round Pond in Hyde Park with no idea how I'd got there, wearing just a T-shirt and jeans and flip-flops in the middle of winter, with no coat, and trying to judge whether the water was deep enough to drown myself. It frightened me so much that I went home and called my parents and asked for help. My parents collected me that night – something I have absolutely no memory of. I was taken home, where I met with my family GP, who prescribed a high dose of Citalopram, and a low dose of Valium to help me adjust to the side effects. I remember absolutely nothing until a week later, when they started to work – even after that, blocks of time are hazy. But they DID work, because I'm still here.'

CHAPTER 8

BODY LANGUAGE

BODY DYSMORPHIA

BODY LANGUAGE

'I felt fat, even though my BMI was fine; I was definitely made to feel that way, not only by others in school, but also by clothes manufacturers as I couldn't find anything to fit me (I was probably a size 12 or 14?). In the end, I just dressed in baggy black clothes.'

A TRUTH:

Everyone hates their body.

Or at least have bits they'd change if they could. Regretfully though, knowing this doesn't make you hate your body any less. Skinny people think they're too bony, tall people think they're too lanky, small people wish they were tall, larger people hate their wobbly bits. Even the super hench muscle boys don't seem satisfied (why else would they be in the gym every day?).

Everyone hates their body.

'Hate' is quite a strong word; most of us have glorious imperfections that we learn to live with, or indeed enjoy. Some of us go and see a doctor to hack, shave, nip, tuck and vacuum out the bits we aren't so keen on, but most of us learn to live with them.

Puberty and adolescence is an especially tough time for the relationship a young person has with their body. The wee child body you're used to starts to morph and change before your very eyes. The process is totally out of your control and cannot be stopped. It's little wonder this is the time various body image issues can start to manifest.

Some consolation can be found in the fact that all young people are going through puberty – you're not alone – and also in understanding that puberty is the ultimate pupa stage: how you look as a teenager will have no bearing on how you'll look as an adult. In fact, I find the funniest-looking teenagers often make the best-looking adults. Hello, that guy who was Neville Longbottom?

GOOGLE FIVE HOT CELEBRITIES WHO LOOKED AWKWARD AS TEENAGERS AND WRITE THEIR NAMES HERE:

1. ....

2. ....

3. ....

4. ....

5. ....

Good job, puberty; good job!

See? There's nothing really to worry about, it's going to be fine. All of us, however, may occasionally experience stress or low mood as a result of how we look. But if such worries become persistent they can start to impact on day-to-day life.

THE TOP 0.001%

At any given time, society creates an ideal standard of beauty that falls within a narrow range. Although much is made of the curvy golden age of Marilyn Monroe, she was still very equally proportioned and her full lips and blonde hair haven't gone anywhere, even if the surprised eyebrows have.

The same is true, to an extent, of men. Although girls have always been bombarded with media representations of female flesh, we have now edged towards a naked gender balance. Films like *Magic Mike* and magazines like *Men's Health* are as damaging for young men as bikini beauty pageants and *FHM* are for young women.

'Magazines did not help at all. In fact, they were part of the problem. Now I think back to the kind of teenage magazines I'd read (with their obsession with weight and beauty) and think that they were downright dangerous. It makes me so angry that, via these channels, I was constantly being told I had to be thin to be liked.'

ANONYMOUS 30 WALES

The problem is that all media (films, books, fashion, magazines and pop videos) converge to spread the beauty lie. The women portrayed are unhealthily thin while maintaining an air of health (and remain booby by way of miracle or plastic implants). They have doll-like faces and big hair. The stick-thin model is still the usual style on the catwalks while tabloids are obsessed with the huge bum – although ONLY the bum can be huge; the waist must remain tiny.

For guys, the idealised silhouette is tall, broad and muscular. Skinnier or chunkier than Michelangelo's *David* is less than ideal. Every once in a while a bigger actor like Chris Pratt will break through only to immediately have to conform to the standard set by his contemporaries and studio bosses. No man is born looking like Chris Hemsworth. To look as buff as him it takes a) four hours a day in the gym, b) an eating disorder – more on that shortly, c) growth steroids or d) a combination of the above.

Of course, there ARE alternative body role models out there, but you have to look pretty hard to find them. Those who do infiltrate mainstream media are often featured in journalism none too subtly mocking how she 'flaunts her curves', accompanied by unflattering long-lens bikini snaps.

As fashion models, Hollywood actors and pop stars represent a tiny proportion of people on the planet, it would be ludicrous to view them as the norm – but it is hard to ignore them. Sometimes it's easy to think they were put on this earth just to make us feel bad about ourselves.

But DO Google them as teenagers. I'll bet they looked vastly different. *This* is a key issue I have with the casting of actors in their twenties to play teenagers on screen: where's the acne? Where are the braces? Where are the ill-fitting fashion choices? These are realities for millions of young people, yet they're all but absent from the media.

A WORD ON ACNE: Bad skin can be crippling for a young person and can lead to very low self-esteem. DO go and see your GP. Most will be sensitive to your plight and can offer medications that can help.

'I was bullied around my physical appearance – spots, argh! – and uncertainty around my sexual orientation.'

To me, teenage years are for figuring out what you'd like to look like as an adult. Some things are movable – while you're at school you have access to free dentistry, for instance – and you can change your hair and clothes as much as you like until you find a style that suits you. I was about twenty-eight before I realised how much a bit of a beard changed my face for the better.

Far more important than what you look like is your health (although looking healthy is nice, obv). Being very overweight or underweight will put strain on your internal organs. We don't want that at all. It's pretty elementary, but every last one of us should work towards a balanced diet with plenty of fruit and veg and enough exercise to keep us vaguely fit. As I've said before, exercise and diet are also hugely important for maintaining your mental health – so what you look like and what you feel like are linked.

BODY DYSMORPHIC DISORDER (BDD): An anxiety disorder that causes a person to have a distorted view of how they look and to spend a lot of time worrying about their appearance. This is NOT the same as vanity. For a sufferer, the tiniest things – a scar, a physical feature, how tanned they are – are disproportionately important and preoccupy their time.

'Eight out of ten women are dissatisfied with their reflection and more than half see a distorted image.'[16]

---

[16] Kate Fox - Social Issues Research Centre

The best we can hope for is an accurate body image and to feel secure with that image. Two very difficult things. It's worth remembering that we see our own bodies differently to how others see us. As individuals we break our body down into component parts – so we are aware of our wonky noses, wobbly bums or spare tyre. However, other people see us as a whole – the little things don't matter to anyone else but us. Various studies also suggest we aren't very good at accurately judging our own size.

While we all have bits we don't like, on-going stresses and anxieties about body image can take a toll on mental and physical health. For some, excessive dieting, obsessive exercise and extreme plastic surgery are symptoms of a deep dissatisfaction. I don't know much, but I know that there's no surgeon's knife for the soul and no one ever weightlifted their way to happiness. Focusing on external attributes is not the path to inner happiness, and never was.

FOOD AND DIET

DR OLIVIA SAYS . . .

Lots of us have a complex or difficult relationship with food, but how do we know when it's time to ask for help? Dieting, calorie counting, meal-skipping and gym regimes are so prevalent it can be hard to know when things have gone too far. That said, it's much easier to break a habit that's been around for weeks than one that's been around for years, so do seek help as soon as you think there may be a problem.

'Complex' is right. Listen to a conversation on a bus or train. Before long, I can almost guarantee talk will turn to food. We're obsessed with the stuff. Granted it keeps us alive, but our preoccupation has gone way beyond that. From 5:2 and Paleo diets to foodies to freegans, we are truly slaves to our next meal.

We have to regard 'eating disorders' as a continuum, the severity dependent on how much of our life is spent worrying about food and the impact on day-to-day living. Too often when people hear 'eating disorder' they think of starvation, but this simply isn't the only story.

At one end of the spectrum we have picky eaters and fad dieters. Given that any doctor would recommend a balanced diet with plenty of fruit and veg, how healthy is any restricted diet? Early in the chapter, I alluded to the 'Buff Diet' – gym bunnies who only eat chicken and protein shakes – this is not eating healthily at all. As we move along the scale, we see 'fasting' diets, compulsive eating, bingeing, purging and eventually starvation.

'I was often berated by my mother for being overweight and for eating anything at all. In 1997 I stopped eating regular meals and lost thirty pounds in two months. I was constantly avoiding eating and was only sleeping and working.'

Although any form of repeated food control can easily develop into a bigger issue there are four recognised official eating disorders:

ANOREXIA NERVOSA

Sufferers will likely be unhealthily preoccupied with food and weight, unable to perceive their own weight accurately and have anxiety around weight gain. The side effects are deadly serious – the strain on the heart is huge and can lead to early death. Other side effects include bone and skin damage and lack of menstruation.

BULIMIA NERVOSA

Sufferers are likely to binge-eat and then obsessively 'compensate' with an activity like vomiting, using laxatives or excessively exercising.

BINGE-EATING DISORDER

Increasingly diagnosed, this condition is defined by two or three periods of extreme binge eating and associated feelings of guilt and shame, but without the 'compensation' activities associated with bulimia nervosa.

OTHER SPECIFIED FEEDING OR EATING DISORDER (OSFED)

This is used by doctors if the other three diagnoses aren't met but there is clear evidence of disordered eating – such as evidence of anorexia – even if weight is still above a healthy level.

DR OLIVIA SAYS . . .

If you were to seek the help of a doctor, they would look at your physical health as well as your mental health. Eating disorders have a HUGE impact on your body. The doctor might therefore also look at your blood pressure and reflexes, as well as checking your height and weight.

If they then had concerns, they would probably refer a patient to CAMHS (if they were under eighteen). Some authorities have specialised eating disorder units.

You would be working with a dietician who would set realistic eating goals with you. They want to help you, not force-feed you.

With eating disorders, although it may appear to be all about food, eating and weight, there are often underlying difficulties that may also need to be worked through.

Let's clear up some myths about eating disorders.

- It's NOT JUST about wanting to be skinny.
- It's NOT JUST about fashion models.
- It's NOT JUST about control.
- It's NOT JUST a fear of food.

By now, the next statement should come as no surprise: eating disorders are a mental illness. As frustrating as it is, not all illnesses have 'a cause'. Although there is some research to suggest there may be a genetic element to diseases like anorexia nervosa, there is also evidence linking such conditions to serotonin imbalance, meaning we can't say an eating disorder is 'caused' by real life any more than depression or anxiety.

This is why, as Dr Olivia suggests, any specialist you see won't just be interested in your food or weight. Simply making a person eat a more balanced diet, although it will help in terms of overall wellness, won't fix the underlying illness.

DR OLIVIA SAYS . . .

Eating disorders are especially tricky as restricting food can lower your appetite. Your behaviour can directly affect your biology. In addition, being undernourished can lead to obsessive thinking or anxiety about food.

'I had a very rocky transition in schooling that I don't feel I was ready for emotionally and I don't think I had enough/any support during this time. It felt very sink or swim and I definitely sank. I've had my eating disorder off and on since my early teens and it is exacerbated by periods of emotional stress – overeating followed by starvation.'

MICHELLE 32 BERKSHIRE

'For most of the latter half of secondary school I self-harmed through an eating disorder, though I was not aware of what I was doing to myself at the time. It was only this year that I analysed what was going on in my mind back then and it was a difficult thing to accept and come to terms with.'

TOM'S STORY

Tom, 29, from London is one of the many thousands of men living with an eating disorder.

'The day started out innocuously enough with a couple of slices of toast and, a bowl of bran flakes, but then I had a row with a friend and, before I knew it, I'd bought, chewed and swallowed two brownies, a bacon sandwich, a packet of crisps, some carrot sticks and a flapjack. Over the next forty-five minutes I added a bag of chocolate buttons, a tuna baguette and a tub of some kind of red and white pudding that looked like someone had pureed a brain and forgotten to pick the skull out. When buying all this, I alternated between a café, a shop and an oh-so-sweetly non-judgemental vending machine, so as not to attract attention.

By now I was sweating, my hands were shaking and I had a pounding headache. I drank about a litre and a half of water, and then I went and had lunch.

When I'm like this, what's driving me isn't hunger, or even the need for comfort, it's the fear that I lack the power over myself to make a binding decision to stop eating. On bad days I feel I can't trust myself, any more than I could a stranger.

The following day I wake up early, feeling like an evil toddler is squatting on my chest. The first thing I do is go for an eight-mile run. At lunchtime I hit the gym and do push-ups and burpees until I want to vomit (but I don't).

I remember the first time a doctor told me I was bulimic. Ironically, I thought he was nuts, because I haven't successfully made myself throw up for more than ten years. I told him this and he said the purge half of my cycle is handled through exercise.

However you characterise it, my relationship with food, my body and the level of control I feel I need over it, is dysfunctional. I also get bouts of depression, am in weekly therapy, and have been on anti-depressants at various points since I was fourteen.

A lot of the time, when people do talk about it, especially celebrities, they cast [bulimia] as a long-past event, a dark episode in their lives ("My year of bulimia hell" etc.). It's the dip in their story arc, a single crisis struggled through in pursuit of their inspirational journey.

Maybe that is what it's like for them, but it's not what it's like for me. For me it's a chronic thing, like diabetes, say. The severity varies from day to day; it comes and it goes, it needs thinking about, and consciously managing, but I can live with it, and live well.'

The full version of Tom's story can be found on his website, tompollock.com/2015/01/08/talking_and_living/

SUPPORT FROM BEAT

As well as talking to a school counsellor or GP, there are online services like The Site and charities like Beat. Beat is the UK's leading charity for eating disorders or difficulties with food, weight and shape.

There are a number of ways in which a young person who has concerns about their relationship with food can contact Beat. If you're ready to share your difficulties with others, you can do any of the following:

- Email Beat's Youthline at fyp@b-eat.co.uk which is handy if you haven't spoken to anyone about your concerns before and are feeling anxious about talking over the phone
- Call Beat's Youthline on 0345 634 7650 – it is open to anyone under 25.
- Access one of their online support groups, including peer-support sessions led by helpline staff, guest professionals or individuals who have recovered from an eating disorder and who can provide insight and support.
- Explore the message boards – to share your experiences with others, read what others have found useful, and join discussions in a supportive, understanding and safe online environment.

Details of all the above, including how to register, opening hours and online support session times can be found on the Beat website: www.b-eat.co.uk.

Beat is there for anybody, whether they have a diagnosed eating disorder, difficulties with food, weight or shape, or are worried about a family member or friend. Parents, teachers or any concerned adults should call the adult helpline: 0345 634 1414 or email help@b-eat.co.uk.

JULIA'S STORY

Julia suffers from an eating disorder, but is now a young ambassador for Beat.

Q. How old were you when you realised you had a problem with food/eating?

A. I was 19 when my problems started.

Q. How did your issues manifest?

A. For me it began with exercising before bed and then developed into restricting my food intake alongside the exercise. I downloaded an app on to my phone on which I would record everything I ate in a day and all the exercise I had done. This began while I was training to be a dancer at a performing arts college.

Q. Did you seek help?

A. I initially went to the GP when it started but my weight was still healthy so not much was suggested. I returned three months later and was put on anti-depressants and was referred to the eating disorder specialist team.

Q. Did you access any NHS services?

A. I had NHS counselling with my case worker, I had meetings regularly at the beginning with an eating disorder nurse and I had a brief stay on the psychiatric ward at my local hospital.

Q. Which type of support helped the most/least?

A. The stay on the psychiatric ward helped keep me safe when my depression was at its worst. However, one of the doctors there was very triggering with some of his comments, so that was both my most and least helpful support. The counselling has helped and after a year I still rely on my meetings heavily.

Q. In the long term, how do you cope with chronic illness and the possibility of relapse?

A. It is very difficult to deal with relapses. Once I started getting better people stopped being so alert around me, which made it hard for me to confide in them when the relapses happened. I get through them with the support of my partner; I tell him everything and he gives me the support I need while also giving me the space to not take my freedom from me.

Q. What other advice do you have for sufferers?

A. Remember that you are not defined by your illness. Try to remember the things that DO define you and hold on to them – for me, reading is a big part of my life and when things get bad I have been able to turn to reading to ease the suffering. Confide in at least one person, always. The danger of this illness comes in secrets; if you have at least one person that you can always confide in, it will make the journey seem more doable. You will need the support.

GENDER DYSPHORIA

'I went through a period of depression that started around the age of fifteen. I also had some issues relating to gender identity and the two combined led to anxiety and feelings of social alienation.'

Gender dysphoria, or believing your true gender is not the gender you were assigned at birth, is fairly common and isn't a mental illness in itself. Remember, there was a time when being gay or lesbian was considered a mental illness! Things change! However, choosing to live in a different gender often comes with a whole bundle of stresses and strains as society isn't quite as ready for trans people as it should be.

There are stark statistics regarding self-harm, substance abuse and suicide among the trans community, so transitioning is something a lot of people find difficult. As with a lot of the disorders we've mentioned in this chapter, feeling unhappy and trapped in your own body isn't likely to inspire a crazy dance party.

Once people have transitioned (either through medical intervention or not), they are often much happier, but the process is long and laborious, so support is often needed. The first port of call can be the family GP or a school counsellor, although, you guessed it, most cases are referred to CAMHS.

This is not so you can be 'treated' for an 'illness' but so you can get the 'support' you 'need'. Sometimes I don't know how to use quotation marks.

CHAPTER 9

THE LAST TABOO?

SELF-HARM AND SUICIDAL THOUGHTS

THE LAST TABOO?

This chapter will contain precious little sasspiration, I'm afraid. It's not easy to make quips about harming oneself or taking one's life, is it? That said, I don't believe anything is too taboo to discuss. Not talking about things gives them a special, mythical aura and, actually, self-harm is something that affects about 7% of young people. Something that common cannot and should not be taboo or ignored.

SELF-HARM

DR OLIVIA SAYS . . .

Self-harm is a person causing themselves physical harm outside of culturally accepted norms. This is why waxing your legs does not count! People harm in lots of different ways, although some common methods include cutting, burning, hair-pulling and skin-picking.

A WORD ON FIRST AID: Before addressing the underlying issues behind self-harm, it's of more pressing concern that we all have a basic knowledge of first aid and recognise when to seek outside medical help. If a person – you or a friend – has hurt themselves it may be necessary to seek medical help. People may not want to because of concerns about what professionals will say or do, but rest assured the most important thing is to take care (no one is going to lock anyone in an asylum). If an injury is

left untreated, there is a risk of infection, further illness and other unintended complications. Cuts should be kept clean and, if necessary, covered with a plaster and antiseptic. If a cut won't stop bleeding, it may require a stitch or two at Accident and Emergency.

Self-harm is increasingly common and people often have lots of questions about it.

SOME FAQ ABOUT SELF-HARM:

- Why are they doing that?
- Are they trying to kill themselves?
- How does it make them feel better?
- Why are they doing this?
- Are they doing it for attention?
- How can they do that to themselves?
- Doesn't it hurt?
- Do I have to hide every sharp object in the house?
- How can I help someone who's self-harming?
- What if they want to be left alone?
- Will it get better?
- How can I stop?
- Do I have to stop?
- Where's the harm in it?

Let me attempt to answer some of these questions, although, as with so many of the issues in this book, there are no DEFINITE answers. Everyone's experience is unique, even if self-harm itself is not.

WHY ARE THEY DOING THAT?

How long is a piece of string? It CAN be about trying to take control of an out-of-control situation; it CAN be about expressing anger or feelings of self-loathing; it CAN be that a person feels like they have run out of answers.

'It was always pretty much anger and self-loathing that drove me to self-harm . . . I couldn't take out my anger on those who made me angry since they were in a position of power over me, and so I took it out on myself instead – and then hated myself for doing that.'

ARE THEY TRYING TO KILL THEMSELVES?

NO! Although people who self-harm may have suicidal thoughts (like a lot of people do), this is something different. Self-harm is actually about a person trying to make themselves feel better, even though this is a FAULTY coping strategy. Sadly, some people who self-harm accidentally kill themselves.

HOW DOES IT MAKE THEM FEEL BETTER?

Self-harm can be a powerful way of changing brain chemicals. Remember endorphins – the tiny dolphins in your head? Well, they are released in response to pain. This creates a TEMPORARY high, which can make sufferers FEEL they're addressing a problem. While a physical effect, obviously these actions don't tackle the underlying issues a sufferer may have. The biological element to it is what can make self-harm difficult to give up.

ARE THEY DOING IT FOR ATTENTION?

I'd hazard most people self-harming would rather eat a live slug than admit their problem. Self-harm comes with a good degree of shame, secrecy and ridicule. However, if someone is letting you know, this indicates they want some attention. And if someone is HURTING THEMSELVES to get attention, boy, do they need it! This, therefore, is NOT a time where terms like 'attention-seeker' or 'manipulative' are going to be especially helpful. What they need is attention – THE RIGHT KIND of attention. It's time to be a good listener, or find someone who is.

'Throughout my teenage years I truly hated everything about myself, from the way I looked to the way I thought. I criticised myself on a daily basis and would self-harm whenever I felt that I deserved it, as well as whenever I was feeling a strong emotion that I didn't know how to deal with. I didn't open up to any of my friends or family about what I was feeling because of shame and guilt. I wanted to be perfect, so I felt that the "me" that I portrayed had to seem perfect.'

DOESN'T IT HURT?

Well, duh. For some people, that's the point. Imagine feeling so desperate that feeling pain was better than feeling nothing at all or a different negative feeling.

HOW CAN I HELP SOMEONE WHO'S SELF-HARMING?

You are not responsible for hiding butter knives and toenail clippers. If someone is that determined to hurt themselves they'll find a way. In fact, no one else can be responsible for the behaviour of another. Ever. However, what would be helpful is asking a sufferer what would work FOR THEM. For example, do they want help finding a charity or a professional to talk to? Are there particular triggers that set them off? Is it worse at certain times of day or year? Listen, do not judge, and look after yourself. After all, hearing about self-harm can be hard. You are not an emotional sponge taking on the woes of others.

WHAT IF THEY WANT TO BE LEFT ALONE?

If a sufferer tells you to sling your hook, this is a sign they are not yet in a position of readiness to change. You accept this and make it abundantly clear that you are ready to help as soon as they need you. Keep that channel open and don't be scared to ask again.

WILL IT GET BETTER?

DR OLIVIA SAYS . . .

The honest answer is 'it can get better' but it's going to take a lot of hard work all round – from a sufferer and their support network, whoever that may be – as self-harm is very hard to stop. Of course things can get better if that's what a sufferer wants. No one wants to be harming for the rest of their lives. As people get older, their brains mature and develop, which can help them to resist impulses to self-harm and plan coping strategies more effectively.

HOW CAN I STOP? DO I HAVE TO STOP?

Two very difficult questions. No one HAS to do anything, but you might want to think what your life will be like in a year, five years, ten years. As you well know, there are drawbacks to self-harm: scars – not being able wear what you want, having to explain them to complete strangers and sexual partners. Do you want this to affect your wedding dress choice if you're a bride? Because it will; it really will. That may feel like a long way off, but do you want to be kicking yourself about your choices as a teenager in your late twenties? I know, when you're in the middle of a dark, bleak period, a future can be hard to imagine at all, but there will be one and you may well want to wear a swimsuit. Scars fade, but they're there forever.

So how can you stop if you are motivated to do so? As with all of the issues we've talked about in this book, you're a gazillion times more likely to succeed with a team on your side – a team you trust and a team you can be honest with and which is honest with you. I don't care who's in your team as long as they're on your side and they're working towards your recovery, not against it. GOOOOOOO, TEAM!

Distraction often works as a coping mechanism. It takes your mind and hands off ruminative thoughts of harm and onto something more practical – and also fun! Don't forget, those scampy mind dolphins are released during exercise, so that's a jolly good alternative way of changing the physical state of your brain and releasing the same chemical you would if you were harming.

LIST FIVE ACTIVITIES THAT YOU FIND WORK AS PLEASING DISTRACTIONS:

1. ....

2. ....

3. ....

4. ....

5. ....

KAT'S STORY

Kat started self-harming as a teenager and sought therapy to help her manage her harming.

'What people don't understand about self-harm is that it's like alcoholism or drug dependency – it doesn't go away; you have to learn to cope with it and control your urges to do it. But it will always be there as an option, as the shortest cut (no pun intended) your brain could take to feeling better and in control. People who have self-harmed – or who do – aren't weak. We have to be strong, as once you start, goodness knows where or if you will stop.

The reaction you get to self-harm can be terribly uninformed as well – mostly people either think it's because I was a selfish teenager looking for attention for spurious reasons or that I'm an unexploded bomb they need to be fearful of because OH MY GOD IF THAT'S WHAT SHE DOES TO HERSELF . . . IMAGINE WHAT SHE'S CAPABLE OF.

I don't think my self-harm defines me but I do think quite a few people find it hard to see past as, unlike other mental health problems, it's such a visible reminder of what I feel and have faced that it challenges people when they can't understand it. Often the perception is that it's a failed suicide attempt and it's almost like they don't expect you to be successful or "normal" – as if you're promoting self-harm as something helpful and supportive.

It's not easy to talk to people who love you about it as they worry so much and find the whole situation upsetting – so I've found counselling very helpful: speaking with someone not emotionally involved with my life. People who love you think it must be their fault in some way too – and I can't deal with their perceived guilt if I need to talk myself down.

One important thing I've learned is not to be ashamed of my scars – they are part of who I am and it's not up to me to be apologetic to other people if they feel uncomfortable. Having them on show isn't about flaunting or being provocative – it's my body and I have the right to bare arms (pun intended this time).'

SUICIDE AND SUICIDAL THOUGHTS

Suicide is when a person decides to end their life and subsequently kills themselves. Every year about 800,000 people do this and for every suicide there are estimated ten to forty attempted suicides. This is very sad.

Suicide is slightly more common in men than women, although suicide ATTEMPTS are much more likely in women.

There is a very strong correlation between suicide and pre-existing mental health problems. Half of all suicide cases had reported a depressive episode earlier in their lives. This makes sense as I can only imagine how low and hopeless someone must feel when they decide life isn't worth living. This makes it all the more sad, as we've now seen how mental health problems are treatable. Perhaps if the stigma around mental health weren't so strong, people would feel more secure in asking for help before taking their lives.

Substance misuse and gambling addiction can also precede suicidal behaviour.

DR OLIVIA SAYS . . .

Thoughts about killing yourself can occur with any mental illness or none. Thinking what the world would be like without you is philosophical and quite normal. Problems come when you get repeated, intrusive thoughts about ending your own life. Practitioners worry more when individuals start thinking in detail about the practicalities of how they would kill themselves. This is not a good sign and shows it may be time to start seeking help.

Here's the thing with suicide:

IT'S A PERMANENT SOLUTION TO A TEMPORARY PROBLEM.

You don't hear people with broken wrists threatening to end it all, because they know their wrist will heal. AND SO WILL YOUR HEAD. Even the worst, bleakest periods of depression can be battled out of. There are systems in place to deal with addiction and debt.

There is always light just round the corner, even in the really exceptionally dark tunnels. My old headmaster used to tell us a story in assembly about a marathon runner who was ready to collapse at the twenty-fifth mile. He couldn't go on, let alone run. But he asked himself, *can I do one more step*? He found that he could. He repeated the question: *can I do one more step*? Before he knew it, taking one painful step at a time, the finishing line was in sight.

THE SAMARITANS: 116 123

There to listen 24 hours a day,
7 days a week,
365 days a year.

CHAPTER 10

PSYCHO

PERSONALITY DISORDERS

PSYCHO

TV shows, films and books have long done a great disservice to mentally ill people. I still occasionally see modern-day depictions of patients being tied to beds in mental health facilities. **THIS DOES NOT HAPPEN.** It's something of a fire hazard, not to mention a breach of human rights.

Like a lot of things, reality just doesn't make for very good entertainment. It's much more fun to have schizophrenic Norman Bates in *Psycho* dress up as his mother and kill shower ladies than it is to show him taking his meds, managing a pleasant motel, attending weekly group therapy and living a very ordinary life with his wife and child.

Far too often, people with mental health problems in films are either cunning, twisted, scheming villains with plans for world domination or raging, angry psychopaths. This isn't the reality of psychosis or personality disorders at all.

While at university, Dr Olivia and I had great fun trying to work out which personality disorders our various friends had. However, there is a clear distinction between a personality TRAIT and a personality DISORDER. A trait becomes a disorder when it is persistent, pervasive and inflexible, continues over time, leads to upset, and has an impact on everyday functioning. Everyone will, from time to time, exhibit TRAITS from the list, but a disorder is something else entirely.

Let's look at some common personality disorders in alphabetical (ish) order!

A IS FOR ANGER MANAGEMENT

Not just for Naomi Campbell. See conduct disorders.

A IS ALSO FOR ANTISOCIAL PERSONALITY DISORDER

Which is basically not giving a sh*t. Characterised by having little regard for safety of self or others, being consistently irresponsible and lacking remorse.

A IS ALSO FOR AUTISTIC SPECTRUM DISORDER (ASD)

DR OLIVIA SAYS . . .

We aren't completely certain what causes autistic spectrum disorders, although there is a genetic component.

ASD is defined by difficulties in social communication, developing and maintaining relationships and a limited or repetitive pattern of interests and activities. It comes under mental illness, although we believe everyone exists on a continuum with regards to ASD. All of us will have some signs, traits or symptoms.

This does not mean having a tidy bedroom, precisely sharpened pencils or a dislike of olives makes a person autistic. *Rain Man* didn't do sufferers any favours by suggesting all ASD people will have a magical power, not unlike one of the X-Men.

What it DOES mean, is that someone with ASD might have difficulty understanding their own and other people's emotions, making friends, and making changes to routine.

A IS ALSO FOR AVOIDANT PERSONALITY DISORDER

Sufferers are disproportionately sensitive to criticism, leading them to avoid social interactions and to persistent feelings of inadequacy.

B IS FOR BIPOLAR DISORDER

Formerly known as manic depression.

DR OLIVIA SAYS . . .

People with bipolar disorder experience highs (mania) and lows (depression) in their mood. Generally, these changes happen over a long time – weeks or months – rather than dramatic ups and downs over the course of a day. Mania can be very frightening as people's thoughts can feel out of control and their behaviour can seem strange to others.

B IS ALSO FOR BORDERLINE PERSONALITY DISORDER

My university favourite because of the accompanying Madonna song. It's actually marked by unstable relationships with others and impulsivity.

C IS FOR CONDUCT DISORDERS

DR OLIVIA SAYS . . .

We are all somewhat prone to anger, aggression, lying, annoying and blaming. However, when this behaviour happens frequently or starts landing us in trouble with others (including the police), people can be diagnosed with conduct disorders.

If behaviour is getting people in bother with the authorities – teachers or police – they may be referred to a youth offending team. These are multi-disciplinary teams that will work with an individual and the people around them to help them manage their issues.

Very often, the team will look into the young person's peer group and family background and try to understand why a person is so unable to control their impulses. Engaging sufferers in meaningful activities is a good way to reduce aggression and antisocial behaviour and build self-esteem.

D IS FOR DEPENDENT PERSONALITY DISORDER

Beyond merely 'clingy', sufferers are submissive, and need to be taken care of, which limits their day-to-day life.

D IS ALSO FOR DEPERSONALISATION

This is when an individual has a recurring feeling of being detached from themself. Imagine feeling like a back-seat driver in your own life, or that there's a veil between you and reality. This is clearly a distressing thing to experience.

'Pretty much every day I would feel like either I wasn't real or the world wasn't real. I'd feel like there was a screen in front of me, like I was trapped in my own body, like I was on a movie set, like the world was made of cardboard.'

D IS ALSO FOR DISSOCIATIVE IDENTITY DISORDER

Despite what you may have seen in films, on TV and in books, developing alternate personalities – two or more distinct characters in the one body – is PHENOMENALLY RARE. In fact, there are very few recorded cases in the world.

H IS FOR HISTRIONIC PERSONALITY DISORDER

People with this disorder are likely to be very dramatic and suggestible and consistently draw attention to themselves.

N IS FOR NARCISSISTIC PERSONALITY DISORDER

An exaggerated sense of self-importance and need for admiration. Sufferers believe they are special and unique but lack empathy towards other people. It becomes a problem when a person struggles to form healthy relationships.

O IS FOR OBSESSIVE-COMPULSIVE PERSONALITY DISORDER

This is not the same as OCD. These people are preoccupied with orderliness, control and perfectionism. As we discussed earlier, OCD is about a lot more than just these things.

O IS FOR OVERACHIEVING

Clinical perfectionism is now recognised as a personality disorder. It can make it difficult to try new things because of the fear of failure or a constant sense of not being good enough.

'I was a top-set sort of kid and the pressure to achieve caused me a lot of stress and depression – I never felt like my best was good enough – and that would send me into a spiral of loathing.'

ANONYMOUS 27 DURHAM

'There was always immense pressure for me to perform well at school, and I tended to experience a lot of self-loathing if I ever performed sub par. I've always had the impression that the only thing I had going for me was that I was a "gifted child", and if I couldn't even perform well in school then what good was I?'

P IS ALSO FOR PARANOID PERSONALITY DISORDER

Being extremely suspicious and mistrusting of others and worrying other people are trying to hurt or deceive.

P IS ALSO FOR POST-TRAUMATIC STRESS DISORDER (PTSD)

Classified as an anxiety disorder, this can manifest following a traumatic event, although not everyone who goes through a traumatic event automatically suffers PTSD. PTSD is usually diagnosed by flashbacks, tactics to avoid re-experiencing the trauma or even discussing it, emotional numbing or memory loss. As with many conditions, there is a measurable chemical change in the brain following trauma and the subsequent fear of it recurring, so it can be treated with medication.

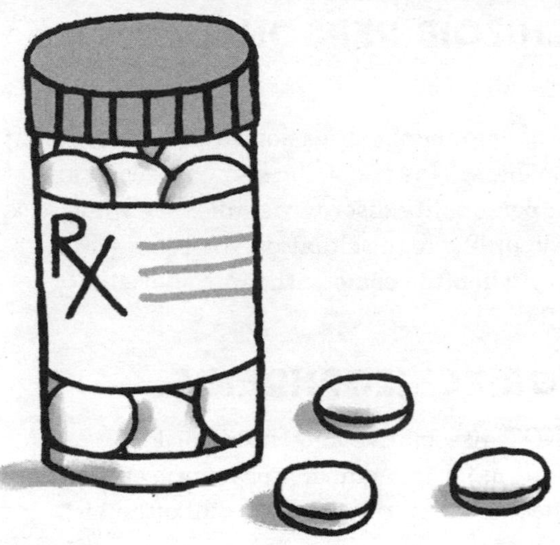

P IS FOR PSYCHOSIS

DR OLIVIA SAYS . . .

Psychosis is a combination of hearing things, seeing things and believing things that other people cannot. For example, a sufferer might be quite convinced that people are trying to hurt them or listen to their conversations. People may have a one-off episode, which can be treated with medication or may resolve itself, but for other people these symptoms persist and can become a chronic illness.

S IS FOR SCHIZOID PERSONALITY DISORDER

A restricted range of emotional expressions and a detachment from social relationships. This is not the same as social anxiety or ASDs because a personality disorder is inflexible while social anxiety fluctuates according to the situation you're in. ASDs are different too as they will often come with characteristic communication difficulties.

S IS ALSO FOR SCHIZOPHRENIA

Schizophrenia is NOT dissociative identity disorder. Schizophrenia is a term for an enduring psychotic episode. Sufferers tend to have poor motivation and will often lack insight into their mental state.

CHAPTER 11

ABOUT ADDICTION

WASTED

Compared to other parts of Europe, the UK isn't doing so well when it comes to drug use. According to a 2011 survey[17], 26% of 15 to 16-year-old boys and 29% of girls the same age in the UK had been on a binge-drinking sesh at least three times in the previous month (for the purpose of the study, binge drinking was classed as having more than five alcoholic drinks in a row). In the same survey, 42% of boys and 35% of girls admitted they had tried illegal drugs at least once.

According to another survey[18], 40% of fifteen-year-olds in the UK have tried cannabis. This number is higher than anywhere else in Europe. The UK was also found to have the joint highest number of young cocaine users, alongside Spain.

Now, while only a reported 0.4% of under-eighteens access services for drugs and alcohol misuse[19], this still represents about 20,000 young people and, as we know by now, those actually SEEKING HELP are likely to just be the tip of the iceberg.

---

[17] The European School Survey Project on Alcohol and Other Drugs, 2011
[18] European Monitoring Centre for Drugs and Drug Addiction, 2014
[19] NHS Substance Misuse Among Young People, 2012

The relationship between addiction and illness is a complex one. Addiction is in itself an illness – habits can form over any stimulus that reinforces itself (meaning, feels good). In some ways we could even look at the neutralising thoughts an OCD sufferer experiences as an addiction – those behaviours are their own rewards.

More complex though is that some people may become addicted to substances or behaviour because of pre-existing health or mental health problems. For example, remember Sam, our OCD sufferer? He uses alcohol as one way of dealing with his condition. One problem then compounds another.

That's all quite tricky to get your head around but, to me, it's quite simple. Substance misuse and mental health issues probably aren't a winning combo.

DR OLIVIA SAYS . . .

We've already seen how our brain chemistry can be affected by mental illness. Drinking alcohol or taking drugs also affects our brain chemistry. While sometimes drugs and alcohol can give us a short-term lift, or make us feel more confident, in the medium to long term, it has a negative affect on our mental health.

I'm not here to be Judge Judy – some drugs are perfectly legal once you turn eighteen, and we mustn't forget that all medications (including the ones we've talked about in this book) have the potential to be dangerous if taken incorrectly. I've always believed that knowledge is power, so let's take a look at some common drugs.

Before we do though, I think it's handy to know what to do if you or someone you know has had a lot to drink or taken a drug, because the MOST IMPORTANT thing is safety.

IF SOMEONE HAS HAD TOO MUCH TO DRINK:

The most important thing is that you keep an eye on a friend who is very drunk. Keep them safe and ensure they get home. Do not let them sleep alone as choking on vomit is a risk. With this in mind, keep them in the recovery position (on their side with their head turned to the side). If they appear to be having any difficulty breathing, call an ambulance at once.

Alcohol poisoning is extremely dangerous. It can lead to a coma and, in extreme cases, death. The amount of alcohol it takes to cause alcohol poisoning depends on many factors, including the person's size, weight, age and so on. Teenagers and inexperienced drinkers are particularly vulnerable.

IF SOMEONE HAS TAKEN DRUGS:

If a friend is having a bad trip (having a panic attack, having difficulty breathing, is 'out of it'), the most important thing you can do is stay calm and stay with them. Try to find out what they've taken but don't stress them out further. It might be helpful to take them outside for fresh air. DO NOT put them in a bath or give them coffee because the bodily changes can cause the body to go into shock.

If your friend is unresponsive, unconscious or having difficulty breathing, you must call an ambulance at once. Telling the paramedic what they have taken is vital and won't be passed to the police.

DIFFERENT DRUGS

So, now we've cleared that up, let's get our facts straight. In simple terms, drugs fall into three categories:

- **uppers/stimulants:** increase alertness, wakefulness and movement
- **downers/depressants:** have a sedative or relaxing effect
- **hallucinogens:** create changes in perception and consciousness

Obviously drugs (legal or otherwise) cost money. Prices may vary, but developing a drug habit can be an expensive affair. Alongside the physical damage done to the body, many users get into debt and trouble with the law by turning to crime to fund a habit.

Now let's look at the most common drugs you've probably heard about and examine what each is doing to your mind and body.

ALCOHOL

'Alcohol is not your friend if you are depressed, and especially not if you think that the world isn't real.'

JENNY 22 LONDON

'I can see that I was using drinking as a means of coping, which did not help me in the slightest. I think that drinking when you are down or anxious about something, in a bad situation or trying to avoid complications of life, will inevitably make you behave in a way that increases any problems with your mental health. I would get drunk and harm myself or become violent to others; I put pressure on people who were good influences in my life. I would contact people that I knew were bad for my mental state, and put myself in situations that meant when I was sober again I would experience the worst downs of my life, and to make it worse I felt I only had myself to blame.'

Here's the thing with alcohol: it's a drug. It's addictive. It's super bad for your health. We know these things and yet there is no more socially accepted non-prescription drug. In fact, NOT drinking is considered socially weird. I'm not going to pretend I don't drink alcohol, I do – although certainly a lot less than I used to for a number of reasons.

The UK has a horrible reputation for binge drinking and antisocial behaviour. While our Mediterranean neighbours sensibly sip wine and grappa over dinner, we're preloading bottles of vodka and coke before going out to drink seven pints of cider and black. With shots on the side. What's interesting is

that our parents and their parents didn't drink to excess in the way subsequent generations seem to.

I don't know if there's a societal reason for our unhealthy relationship with booze, or if, in fact, we're being exploited by the drinks industry and the government (who make a packet on alcohol tax), but one thing's for sure: if we keep drinking the way we do, we're heading for a generation of people with drink-related illnesses in their thirties and forties.

Although you have to be over eighteen to purchase alcohol in the UK, it is very common for teenagers to start much younger than that as peer pressure to partake in the demon drink is pretty much normalised.

PEER PRESSURE: External pressure from a social group (friends or schoolmates) to try a new substance or activity. The desire to fit in is powerful and no one wants to lose face or status, but if your head is telling you something is a bad idea, you should always trust your instincts. Saying NO won't may you look loserly, it'll make you look like a free-thinking individual who isn't a blind follower.

What does alcohol do to your body?

In the short term, alcohol affects coordination, but sustained use and binge drinking will start to damage your organs. The heart, liver, pancreas and bowel can all be affected by alcohol and drinking too much is linked to various cancers of the mouth, throat, stomach and breasts. Drinking can also affect your chances of having a baby whether you're male or female – it reduces fertility.

What does alcohol do to your brain?

Alcohol is a depressant, so it slows the functioning of your brain. Initially this can feel pleasing, but can quickly lead to blackouts, loss of memory and depressed feelings.

'When I did drink, I drank quite heavily. I enjoyed how it made me feel and that I didn't have to worry about my anxieties any more and I felt like I could be more social with people I wouldn't otherwise want to talk to. I don't feel like it negatively impacted my health.'

'At first drinking would block everything out; it made it easier for me to behave "normally" and talk to people. But then I started to get depressed when I drank.'

I'll be honest about drinking, it's not sexy. Okay, smizing coquettishly over a glass of champagne is one thing, vomming in a gutter and trying to snog someone covered in lager and carrot chunks is quite another.

SMOKING AND NICOTINE

Since smoking in public places was banned in 2007, the number of smokers has sharply dropped as no one really likes huddling under a heat lamp in a rainy beer garden or wee-scented doorway. That said, the advent of vaping may be about to reverse it all again. But is vaping any better for you? The chemicals in e-cigarettes are much the same as those in cigarettes, minus the harmful smoke, and are just as addictive. It is illegal to purchase cigarettes (of any sort) under the age of eighteen in the UK.

What does smoking do to your body?

When you inhale smoke, toxins enter your bloodstream. These toxins narrow your arteries, and increase your blood pressure and chance of blood clots and heart attacks. The lungs take the worst hit: 84% of lung cancer patients are smokers, but smokers are also more likely to be bronchitis, asthma and emphysema sufferers. Smokers will also suffer reproductive issues, poor skin quality, a reduced sense of taste and a massively increased risk of mouth, throat and stomach cancers. Hmmm, sign me up.

What does smoking do to your brain?

Nicotine (and the other chemicals found in cigarettes) is a stimulant and provokes a temporary high when people first start smoking. Very quickly the smoker gets used to it and no longer experiences the high; instead they need a cigarette solely to diminish the negative effects of craving one. Smoking also makes the chances of having a stroke or brain aneurism much higher.

The good news is as soon as you stop smoking (and the younger you stop) the more chance your body has of fixing itself. So stop now, because your body can't repair being dead.

I'll be honest about smoking. It's not sexy. You might think it's sexy because Audrey Hepburn and James Dean smoked on the silver screen like a hundred years ago, but in reality it's more Dot Cotton or Nigel Farage than Lauren Bacall. People who smoke smell – like, really, REALLY smell. If smokers tell you this is not true, it's because their sense of taste and smell has been destroyed by the habit. Kissing a smoker is also, as my granddad used to say, like 'kissing a chimney'. He's not wrong.

CANNABIS

'Marijuana did not impact my mental health – it probably improved it. Each time I did it, I was with friends in a safe environment and it served for entertainment, nothing else.'

ALESSANDRA 21 PARAGUAY

'I experimented with cannabis twice and both times the disassociation and anxiety caused by the drug use, though not traumatic, convinced me that, with my mental health issues, drugs are not something to be tried ever again (though that is just me personally). I struggle enough with my brain being irrational on a good day; I don't need a mind-altering substance to disconnect me from objective reality even more.'

Oh, who to believe? Some users find cannabis brings about a chilled-out feeling but, unless it's prescribed medicinally, cannabis is still an illegal Class B drug.

Cannabis is derived from the leaves and resin of the cannabis plant and can be smoked or eaten. Your may have heard of this drug referred to as marijuana, pot, puff or skunk. Skunk is a slightly different, much stronger variation.

What does cannabis do to your body?

As cannabis is usually smoked, it has all the same negative side effects as smoking, as most users mix the cannabis with tobacco. Users may also get 'the munchies', a sudden hunger that can lead to weight gain. Sometimes people pull 'a whitey' when they become nauseous and vomit.

What does cannabis do to your brain?

Cannabis is a downer, which can make a user feel relaxed and chilled out. Although not officially addictive, some studies show the drug is highly habit-forming on a psychological level. It can also be hallucinogenic – you may see or hear things that aren't real. It makes some users feel anxious or panicky. Some studies show that repeat users lack motivation, display lower brain functioning and perform poorly on tests.

DR OLIVIA SAYS . . .

There is a link between cannabis use and psychosis. At the moment, we don't know whether people who are vulnerable to psychosis are more likely to use cannabis or whether using cannabis can cause the symptoms of psychosis.

Currently we think that for some people who are predisposed to developing psychosis, smoking or taking cannabis can lead to the first symptoms developing. This is called the 'stress-vulnerability hypothesis'. What we do know is that for people who go on to develop psychosis it is a frightening illness that can develop into a chronic condition, such as schizophrenia.

I'll be honest about repeated pot smoking. It's not sexy. Nobody that mashed off their face all the time is sexy. People who are high are both a) irritating and b) a bit zombiefied. And they also smell.

MEDICATION

You know this by now, but ALL DRUGS ARE BAD DRUGS unless you stick to your prescription. That's right, even the seemingly innocent paracetamol can be deadly when overdosed. In fact, overdosing on painkillers is a sure way to destroy your liver and kidney – many people who try to commit suicide this way instead wind up with long and painful chronic illnesses.

Some medications, like codeine and sleeping tablets, can be habit-forming, so you have to be especially careful with such medicines and listen closely to advice from your GP.

COCAINE

Otherwise known as coke, charlie and, in its cooked form, crack. Usually inhaled as a white powder or smoked as 'rock', cocaine is highly, highly addictive and is an illegal Class A drug. It has a similar effect to amphetamines (speed) or crystal meth (methamphetamine).

Coke is a powerful stimulant that gives a short-lived 'high' during which a user will feel confident, clever, alert and invincible. This is often followed by an unpleasant comedown.

What does cocaine do to your body?

Coke raises your heartbeat and temperature. Sometimes when people overdose they have a heart attack as a result. You may have also seen certain high-profile cases of noses decaying from repeated cocaine use. Yep! Noses actually dropping off! That said, nose bleeds with little lumps of nose tissue are much more common, so that's okay. (*wtf face*)

What does cocaine do to your brain?

Coke is an 'upper', which means users will experience a short-lived high, or sense of euphoria. This is caused when the drug blocks reuptake of serotonin in your brain – meaning you have a higher than usual level of the happy-making chemical in your head.

I'll be honest about cocaine. It's not sexy. Unless you find hugely self-involved high-speed conversations about utter jibberish sexy, it's a no-no. People on coke are deeply, deeply irritating.

HEROIN

Often called smack, junk or gear. Once considered the drug of choice for sketchy hobos and prostitutes, in recent years there have been high-profile heroin deaths of famous people, such as actor Philip Seymour Hoffman and TV personality Peaches Geldof.

Oh, this is a horrible, horrible drug. There's nothing romantic, wistful or poetic about heroin. It isn't 'rock and roll'. It's monstrously addictive and the chance of infection and overdose is painfully high. Just read Melvin Burgess's *Junk* and let me know if you fancy a bit of smack. I can guarantee the answer will be NO.

Heroin is derived from a poppy-extract painkiller called morphine, although it's very often 'cut' with other substances like sugar, starch, paracetamol or brick dust. In its heroin form it is an illegal Class A drug.

What does heroin do to my body?

Mostly a user will feel sleepy after taking heroin. However, it's very easy to overdose on. Most heroin deaths are from respiratory failure. Common side effects include collapsed veins, weight loss and gangrene. There is also an ever-present risk of HIV or hepatitis infection if needles are shared with other users.

What does heroin do to my brain?

Heroin works like an painkiller – it dulls the receptors of the nervous system. This gives an impression of warmth and relaxation. Heroin is hugely addictive.

I'll be honest about heroin. It's not sexy. Clearly. No one likes collapsed veins and gaunt faces. There's no such thing as 'heroin chic'.

ECSTASY

Ecstasy is a name for MDMA, which can be taken as pills or powder, and was the dance drug of the nineties. It's a stimulant that helps a user stay up all night, feel energised and want to hug people indiscriminately. Ecstasy is an illegal drug and very often what a user is sold is NOT pure MDMA as pills can be mixed with other substances or are something else entirely (pet worming tablet, anyone? No?). There is a risk of overdosing if the first pill doesn't make them 'come up' or in mistaking the much deadlier PMA for MDMA.

What does ecstasy do to my body?

Ecstasy is an upper and a stimulant. Physical side effects include increased heart rate, dilated pupils and a tell-tale tightening of the jaw, or gurning.

What does ecstasy do to my brain?

Another drug that messes with the chemicals in your brain. This one releases a burst of serotonin and dopamine, giving a feeling of euphoria.

I'll be honest about ecstasy. It's not sexy. You might be feeling the love, but you look like a bulldog chewing a wasp.

HALLUCINOGENS

For some, the symptoms of psychosis prove irresistible (again, *wtf face*) and they turn to drugs like acid (LSD) or psilocybin (magic) mushrooms to bring about a 'trip'. Now, a good trip can be fun or amusing, but a bad trip is, quite literally, a living nightmare.

Magic mushrooms also carry a risk of users eating the wrong type of mushroom – some are poisonous. What's more, for people with pre-existing anxiety disorders, mushrooms are much more likely to bring about panic attacks.

What do hallucinogens do to my body?

Both LSD and magic mushrooms alter your vision and hearing, and time can appear to speed up or slow down. Some users vomit or get diarrhoea.

What do hallucinogens do to my brain?

LSD, once again, affects dopamine and serotonin receptors. Magic mushrooms contain a compound called psilocin, which is psychedelic (mind-altering). Sorry, kids, not actually magic.

I'll be honest about magic mushrooms and LSD. In fact, I bet you can guess. They're not sexy. It's very much like being at the cinema where everyone's watching a different film. At least one is watching a very scary horror movie.

LEGAL HIGHS

Just because a high is legal doesn't make it safe; all it means is that it's an unregulated substance, usually not intended for human consumption. Some of them are uppers, some of them are downers, and none of them are truly safe as no one can guarantee what's in them. Often they are advertised as incense, fertiliser or bath salts to get around the law.

Depending on what you've taken, the effect will either be a stimulant (like cocaine, speed or ecstasy), a depressant (like cannabis) or hallucinogenic (like acid or magic mushrooms) and have all the same risks and side effects.

Many previously legal highs, such as the popular mephedrone, ARE now illegal.

GASES

Sniffing or inhaling glue or aerosols is WELL EIGHTIES but the solvents trend seems to be having something of a revival.

You can't go to a festival now without seeing tiny canisters of gas lying around. These contain nitrous oxide, or laughing gas. Previously used only by dentists or in the manufacture of whipped cream, inhaling nitrous oxide creates a dizzy, light sensation but can also cause headaches and death from lack of oxygen to the brain. No laughing matter. Nitrous oxide isn't illegal to possess, but it is a crime to sell it to under-eighteens.

A great number of other household solvents present in glues, aerosols and substances like correction fluid contain volatile chemicals that, when sniffed, act as a depressant. They may cause a dizzy, dream-like sensation but the effect on the heart is so strong they can cause sudden death, or 'sudden sniffing death syndrome' as it's officially known. You can die the first time you try.

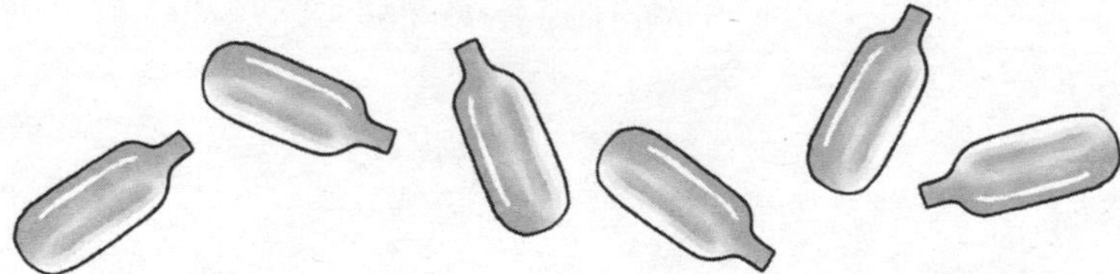

Between 2000 and 2008, more young people died from sniffing solvents than all other illegal drugs combined.

ALCOHOL AND DRUGS AS SELF-MEDICATION

Now that we know all our uppers and downers, it's easy to see why some people with mental health problems would seek to either perk themselves up or calm themselves down, especially if they don't want to access legit mental health services.

DR OLIVIA SAYS . . .

Sometimes mental health problems can make us feel so low or anxious that using chemicals to improve our mood seems like a good idea. This is a short-term solution that can actually make your mental health worse and leave a person with more problems than they started with. Alcohol and drugs can also interact with prescribed medication, with unforeseen complications.

As we've seen, many drugs (illegal or otherwise) can be addictive, expensive and deeply unsexy. As Dr Olivia says, (unprescribed) drugs and alcohol aren't really doing anything to 'fix' you or help you get better. In fact, I'd argue they are a barrier to seeking a healthier form of support.

HOW DO I KNOW IF I'VE GOT A PROBLEM?

A lot of people use a fairly simple **CAGE** system for deciding if they have a problem with drink or drugs. It's easy:

1. **HAVE YOU EVER THOUGHT YOU SHOULD CUT BACK ON DRINK OR DRUGS?** **YES/NO**
2. **DO YOU GET ANNOYED IF PEOPLE QUESTION YOUR DRUG USE/DRINKING?** **YES/NO**
3. **DO YOU FEEL GUILTY ABOUT WHAT YOU DID WHILE DRUNK/HIGH?** **YES/NO**
4. **HAVE YOU DRUNK/DONE DRUGS TO EASE WITHDRAWAL OR A HANGOVER?** **YES/NO**

If you've answered yes to any of these questions, it might be time to reflect on your health, both mental and physical. It doesn't mean you're an addict, but why have drink and drugs become such a large part of your life? I can't imagine it's much fun any more.

CHAPTER 12

LIVING WITH LIFE

GETTING BETTER

LIVING WITH LIFE

So it gets better, right? Like a cough or a cold, one day you wake up and suddenly feel better – that's true of mental health too? Well . . . no. There comes a day in everyone's life when you realise that there are good days and bad days, and then a later realisation that there will also be bad weeks, months and years. However, would you want to be blissfully happy all day, every day? That actually sounds quite tiring. Both highs and lows are temporary. And while a low might last a while, it won't last for ever. It really won't.

DR OLIVIA SAYS . . .

There is no way of saying how long a mental health condition is likely to last for. What we do know is that the quicker a person is treated, the better the outcome. Once you've had one episode of mental health difficulties there is a possibility you'll have another; however, you will now be better at understanding what is happening and be better at seeking the treatment that works for you.

As a teenager your identity is growing and changing as you discover what kind of person you are and who you want to be.

We all try on different identities and self-images over time and discard those things we don't like or that no longer fit us. When people identify very closely with a psychiatric diagnosis – for example, they feel that being 'AN ANOREXIC' is a large part of who they are – this can make moving on and getting better even more difficult.

Whether we see it or not, all of us are made up of multiple identities – a friend, a brother, a sister, an athlete, a lesbian, a bookworm – all of these elements interact, but none wholly define us by themselves. Managing our mental health is one part of our life, but if that's all we have, the funhouse walls will start shrinking in. Our lives will become smaller and smaller, with room only for you and your mental illness.

Dwelling on mental health too much will create a very small world, and quite a gloomy one. That's precisely what mental illness can feel like, and it's something to be fought not cherished.

While we all have foibles, personality traits, down days, manic days, drunk days (if you drink), hungover days (if you drink too much) and mental illnesses, the goal is to live a broad and fulfilling life outside of these things. I refuse to accept that the most interesting about anyone reading this book is the state of their mental health.

FEELING BETTER

Getting better and feeling good is a long-term commitment. Frankly, being alive is a long-term commitment. One thing is for sure, there are no magic wands and as much as we'd like to fall asleep and wake up in a state of perpetual euphoria, it's NEVER gonna happen.

So how do we do it? Well, it's a step-by-step thing. At the start of this book, I asked you what your general mood was like on a scale of one to ten. Let's go again – how are you feeling right now?

1 2 3 4 5 6 7 8 9 10

Awful Awesome

The trick isn't in jumping from 2 to 8 in a miraculous mood swing. If you assessed your mood at 4, the ONLY question is, **what will move you on to a 5?** All of a sudden it doesn't look so hard. If you're a 4, will a cup of a tea and a night in with Netflix get you to a 5? From there, what would get you to a 6? Asking questions like, **but what if I want to be an 8 for ever?** aren't especially helpful because NO ONE is an 8 forever. A better question would be: **under what circumstances could I maintain a positive mood?** I'm afraid these circumstances may well involve you making CHANGES in your life. These might include ending a relationship or changing jobs or schools. It may involve therapy or medication. It may involve something very small like having a talk with someone who's upsetting you.

Another helpful question would be, if you scored yourself a 4: what stopped me from scoring a 3? It is always fruitful to reflect on the positive things in your life as these are hugely important. It can be easier to reflect on pain and hurt – they're loud and noisy. It takes skill and focus to celebrate achievements and affirm ourselves.

Dr Olivia is also right in that as we mature we get used to living in our very imperfect skin. We learn to manage ourselves and know what works for us. We understand what makes us feel comfortable and recognise warning signs when things are going wrong. This means that when we have crises, we are able to better anticipate them and deal with them more effectively – almost to the point that it becomes a boring run-of-the-mill thing.

My anxiety issues are now managed by a healthy supply of Imodium and an emergency 30p for the train-station loo. Just having those things in my bag helps me to manage my problem and carry on with a totally normal life.

Remember that story about the marathon runner who, even when he was ready to collapse, asked himself, can you take one more step? Life is, excuse the metaphor, a marathon. Ask yourself, even in your darkest moment: can you take one more step?

You and I both know the answer is yes.

WHAT HAVE YOU LEARNED?

Test yourself with the crossword on the next page.

ACROSS

1. Not a dog but a. . . ? (Easy one to get you started)
3. Eating disorder in which sufferers binge-eat before purging
6. Charity specialising in listening to people with suicidal thoughts
7. Colour associated with sadness
8. This personality disorder is characterised by dramatic behaviour
10. When someone dies
11. Acronym used to describe most depression or anxiety medications

DOWN

1. Obsessive __________ disorder, otherwise known as OCD
2. Not actually a tiny dolphin in your head
4. Illegal drug, often a white powder
5. Eating disorder charity
6. Very strong form of cannabis
9. Acronym for Children and Adolescent Mental Health Services

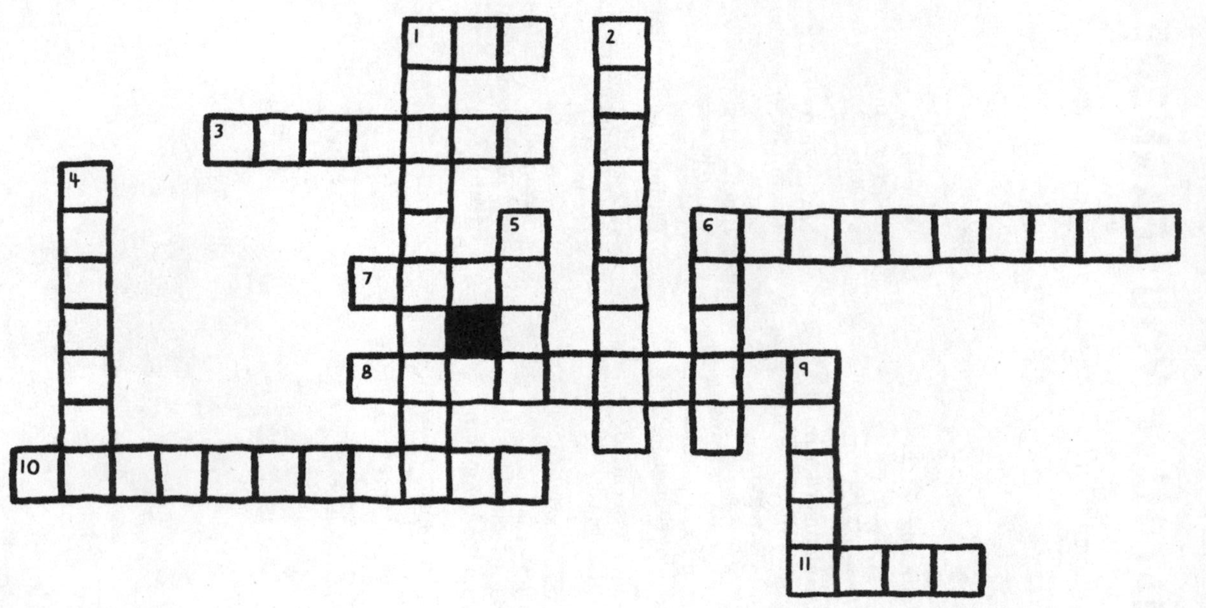
1
2
3
4
5
6
7
8
9
10
11

CHAPTER 13

HELPFUL STUFF

Some handy phone numbers and websites to save you the effort of Googling!

NHS MENTAL HEALTH:

www.nhs.uk/livewell/mentalhealth

CHILDLINE:

Call 0800 1111 or log on to **childline.org** to talk confidentially to an online counsellor 24/7.

SAMARITANS:

Call 116 123 or you can also drop in to a walk-in centre or email a listener. You don't have to be suicidal to call; you can just talk about how you are feeling.

THESITE:

Log on to **TheSite.org** for advice on relationships, money, drugs, sexuality, self-harm and life, plus forums and online counsellors.

BEAT (BEAT EATING DISORDERS):

Helpline 0345 634 1414 or access **b-eat.co.uk** for online support community.

YOUNG MINDS:

youngminds.org.uk gives a great account of what mental services are available to young people and also a helpline for concerned parents: 0808 802 5544.

MIND:

mind.org.uk or 0300 123 3393
For help and information on all areas of mental health, plus access to emergency support.

SWITCHBOARD – THE LGBTQ* HELPLINE:

Providing help to the LGBTQ* community. Helpline 0300 330 0630 (open 10am – 11pm daily). Text message and email support also available, so it doesn't have to show up on a home-phone bill.

FRANK:

talktofrank.com Confidential drugs advice on every drug you can possibly imagine. They also offer a helpline, 0300 123 6600, and live chat online.

ADVICE FOR PARENTS

Worrying that your child is suffering from a mental health problem is awful – not as awful as actually having them, but still pretty bad. It's possible you've experienced mental health issues of your own, or maybe you haven't. Either way, it's important to treat mental illness the same way you would any illness... with sympathy.

Some points to remember:

- It's NOT a cry for attention, and if it is, anyone declaring they have mental health problems is probably in need of the right sort of attention.
- No one ever got better through pestering. You can't badger someone better; these things take time, and often intervention.
- No one likes being cornered. If a person is to be helped, they need to be in the frame of mind to accept help. Forcing a young person to see a doctor against their will could well hinder their recovery.

So what can you do if you have concerns about a young person? The most important thing is to listen to them and believe what they're telling you. If they're not communicating, the tell-tale signs to look out for are:

- recent social withdrawal and loss of interest in friends or stuff they used to enjoy.
- changes at school or college, such as quitting sports teams, failing academically or social problems.
- poor concentration, memory, lack of logical thought and slurred speech.

* loss of initiative or desire to participate in any activity; apathy.
* unusual or exaggerated beliefs about personal powers, paranoia, hallucinations, i.e. hearing or seeing things that others can't.
* dramatic sleep and appetite changes or deterioration in personal hygiene.
* rapid or dramatic shifts in feelings or mood swings.

You'll notice that the vast majority of these traits are present in approximately 98% of teenagers, so good luck with that.

I think the best thing you can do is TALK about the mental wellbeing issues you've read about in this book – demonstrate that you understand the pressures of being a young adult and know what support options are available. Keep channels of communication open at all times and assure them that, when it comes to conversation, nothing is taboo – not contraception, identity or anxieties. DO look at the websites recommended in this section.

Finally, Young Minds offer specialist help for parents. Their helpline number is 0808 802 5544 and in the first instance they'll offer guidance and materials but they also run a call-back service whereby someone from CAMHS will ring you back to discuss the right course of action.

AFTERWORD

Since writing the first draft of *Mind Your Head*, my anxiety issues took a turn for the worse. My schedule and travel anxieties hit critical mass and I ended up having a huge (and very public) panic attack at the Hay Festival in 2015. On stage. With Malorie Blackman. MORTIFYING.

I forced myself to complete my US tour of *This Book Is Gay*, but getting on that plane wasn't easy and I had to cancel an appearance in Connecticut. Sorry, Connecticut.

As soon as I was back on UK soil, I booked an appointment with my GP and, you know what, he was AMAZING. He listened carefully and asked why I hadn't tried SSRIs before to tackle my IBS (which is, as we know, related to anxiety). We agreed they were worth a try.

I was first prescribed sertraline. It did not go well. Within hours I was pooping green oil (I KNOW), gurning like I'd taken all the MDMA in the world and couldn't sleep for three days (and when I did sleep my dreams were INSANE). That said, a dear friend of mine was prescribed sertraline after she left her husband and, once the initial sleepiness had passed, she experienced no side effects and certainly no green poop. But I stopped taking the pills and went back to my GP.

He assured me the side effects would have abated eventually, but sod that: GREEN POOP. He instead prescribed escitalopram, which has been a MARVEL. I get a little dry-mouth but other than that there have been no side effects. What's interesting is that I don't feel massively different but I keep remembering that I've forgotten to stress out about things.

Case in point: I went to see QUEEN TAYLOR OF SWIFT in concert in Hyde Park, London. Before, a day in a park with only

Portaloos would have been inconceivable. I'd have been so worried about there not being access to a bathroom that it wouldn't have been worth going. However, on my way home it occurred to me I hadn't even thought to worry! Amazing!

They have made a real difference. It's not like HALLELUJAH, I'M CURED but things are certainly a lot easier and, vitally, I'm learning to enjoy life again, free from worry. Sometimes it's only when you're a bit better that you even realise things were bad.

Previously I would have been reluctant to start on medication, but actually the results have been so positive that I'm quite happy to continue for the time being. I also see a therapist and we'll carry on discussing why I got so anxious in the first place.

Looking after your mental health is no different from going to a gym or trying to eat your five a day. It's maintenance. I wish I'd taken the time to mind my head before things got so bad, as prevention is better than cure, but I very much pretended everything was fine when it wasn't.

So be mindful; talk to one another; eat and sleep well and don't ever be afraid to ask for help. It's all part of being human.

Juno

xxx

HELP

INDEX

BIBLIOGRAPHY

Parsons, T *The Social System* Glencoe, IL: The Free Press, 1951

Blumenthal JA, Babyak MA, Doraiswamy PM, Watkins L, Hoffman BM, Barbour KA, Herman S, Craighead WE, Brosse AL, Waugh R, Hinderliter A, Sherwood A 'Exercise and pharmacotherapy in the treatment of major depressive disorder' *Psychosomatic Medicine* 2007

J. Thompson Coon, K. Boddy, K. Stein, R. Whear, J. Barton, and M. H. Depledge 'Does participating in physical activity in outdoor natural environments have a greater effect on physical and mental wellbeing than physical activity indoors?' *Environmental Science and Technology* 2001

Holmes, T and Rahe, R. Holmes-Rahe 'Social readjustment rating scale' *Journal of Psychosomatic Research Vol II* 1967

Aldwin, CM *Stress, Coping and Development* Guildford Press, 2007

Seligman, M *Learned Optimism* New York: A. A. Knopf, Inc., 1990

Seligman, M *Helplessness: On Depression, Development, and Death* San Francisco: W.H. Freeman, 1975

Carlson, NR & Heth, CD *Psychology: the science of behaviour. 4th ed.* Upper Saddle River, New Jersey: Pearson Education, Inc., 2007

CROSSWORD ANSWERS

ACROSS

1. Cat
3. Bulimia
6. Samaritans
7. Blue
8. Histrionic
10. Bereavement
11. SSRI

DOWN

1. Compulsive
2. Endorphin
4. Cocaine
5. Beat
6. Skunk
9. CAMHS

ACKNOWLEDGEMENTS

Thank you to . . .

All the people who shared their stories for this book. Imagine all the people who will feel less alone because you were brave enough to tell your tales.

To Olivia, one of my oldest friends, for helping me get it right.To Gemma for the gorgeous illustrations. To everyone at Hot Key Books for everything.

To you, the reader, for helping me spread a very simple message: We all need help sometimes, never be afraid to ask for it. You don't ask, you don't get.

ABOUT JUNO DAWSON

Queen of Teen 2014 Juno Dawson is the multi award-winning author of dark teen thrillers *Hollow Pike*, *Cruel Summer*, *Say Her Name* and *Under My Skin*. In 2015, she released her first contemporary romance, *All of the Above*. Her first non-fiction book, *Being a Boy* tackled puberty, sex and relationships in a frank and funny fashion. A follow up for young LGBT people, *This Book is Gay* came out in 2014.

Juno is a regular contributor to *Attitude* magazine, *GT*, *Glamour* and the *Guardian* and has contributed to news items concerning sexuality, identity, literature and education on BBC Women's Hour, Front Row, This Morning and Newsnight. She is also a School Role Model for the charity STONEWALL and works with charity First Story to visit schools serving low income communities. Juno's titles have received rave reviews and her books have been translated into more than ten languages.

In 2015, Juno announced her transition to become a woman, having lived thus far as the male author James Dawson. She writes full time and lives in Brighton.

Follow Juno on Twitter @junodawson
or Facebook as Juno Dawson Books

ABOUT GEMMA CORRELL

Illustrator Gemma Correll is one of the few people in the universe who has managed to turn her love of pugs into a lucrative career. She has exhibited all over the world — in China, the US and Europe — and was the recipient of a Young Guns award from the Art Directors Club of New York in 2010. She's a serial punner with a crush on all things cartooney and studied graphic design in Norwich. Her favourite colour is turquoise, her star sign is Aquarius and her favourite word is 'Albuquerque', just in case you were wondering.

Follow Gemma on Twitter: @gemmacorrell

ABOUT DR OLIVIA HEWITT

Dr Olivia Hewitt is a clinical psychologist who has worked in the NHS since 2003. After meeting co-author Juno Dawson while at university in north Wales she went on to train at the University of Oxford. Since then she has specialised in working with people with a learning disability, as well as writing for academic journals and lecturing at the universities of Southampton and Oxford. Outside work, Olivia can be found reading detective novels and helping out on the farm. She lives with her husband in Oxfordshire.

HOT
KEY
BOOKS